A CHILD'S
BIBLE

First published 1969 in two volumes by
Wolfe Publishing Ltd
Piccolo two-volume edition published 1973
by Pan Books Ltd,
London
This revised one-volume edition
published 1986
Designed and edited by Treld Bicknell
Calligraphy by Charles Front
© Pan Books Ltd, 1973
Published by Paulist Press in the
United States of America
997 Macarthur Boulevard
Mahwah, New Jersey 07430
ISBN: 0-8091-2867-5
Printed and bound in Spain by
Mateu Cromo Artes Gráficas, S. A. Pinto (Madrid)

A CHILD'S BIBLE

THE OLD TESTAMENT

Re-written for children by
Anne Edwards

Illustrated by
Charles Front & David Christian

THE NEW TESTAMENT

Re-written for children by
Shirley Steen

Illustrated by
Charles Front

Paulist Press
New York / New Jersey

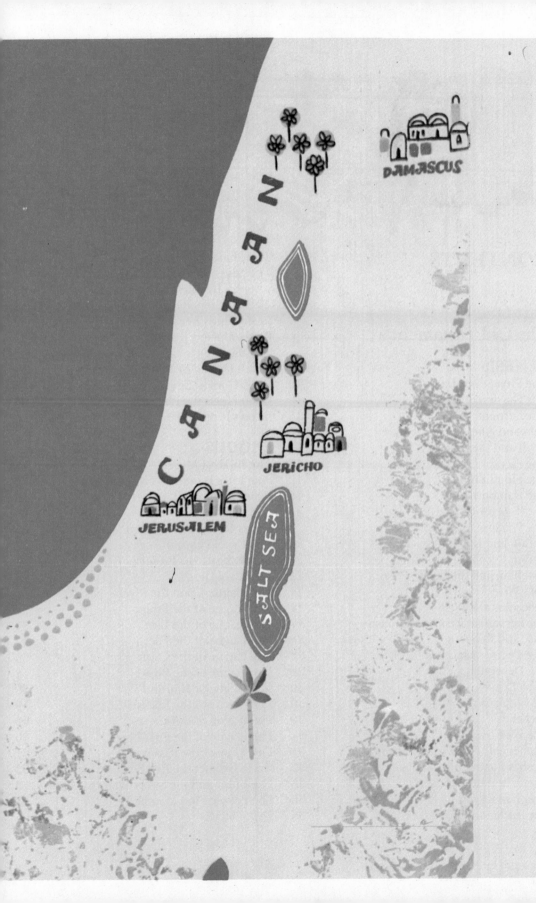

CONTENTS

Part One:
The Old Testament

Part Two:
The New Testament

THE OLD TESTAMENT

GENESIS

The First Seven Days

In the beginning there was no heaven and no earth and no darkness and no light and so God said, 'Let there be light,' and there was light. And He called the light Day ... and the darkness, Night. And that was the first day.

But when the light came up on the second day, God could see that His work was not done and so He said, 'Let there be a sky,' and there was a sky!

On the third day God could see He *still* had more work to do and so He created the dry land which He called the earth and the water which He called the seas, and very quickly there were grass and plants and trees with lovely fruits.

On the fourth day God added to the sky the sun and the stars so that there would *always* be light.

And on the fifth day there was so much beauty that God added living things to make it *really* complete. He created great whales and small fishes and birds that could fly above the green trees and the rich earth and the deep blue seas.

God could see that all of this was good and beautiful and so, on the sixth day, He added every kind of animal – and then He created man!

By the seventh day God was tired from all this work, so He rested and blessed the seventh day and made it a day for all living things to rest.

And then, when God had rested, long enough, He planted a garden eastward in a place called Eden and there He put the man whom He had made.

•

The Garden of Eden

The Garden of Eden had every tree that was pleasant to behold and which bore good fruit to eat. But God planted two other trees in the Garden of Eden – one was the Tree of Life and the other was the Tree of Good and Evil – and, when

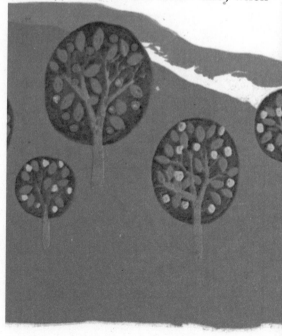

the Lord God put the man in the Garden of Eden, He told him he was to care for the garden and for his work he could eat from any tree *except* from the Tree of Good and Evil – for if he ate from that he would surely die! And He called the man Adam, but Adam – even with all the trees, the birds, and the animals – was lonely.

So one night, while Adam slept, God took one of Adam's ribs and from this rib He made a woman. And, when Adam woke the next morning, God brought her to Adam and told him she would be called woman because part of her came from man. The woman became Adam's wife and Adam named his wife, Eve.

•

Genesis 3

The Serpent

There was in the garden a serpent who was very evil and he asked Eve, 'Did God forbid you to eat the fruit of the trees in the garden?'

'No,' Eve answered, 'we are only forbidden to eat the fruit on the tree in the middle of the garden. God said we would die if we did so.'

'You will not die,' the evil serpent told her.

And so Eve was tempted to eat the rich red fruit on the forbidden tree. And when she did she felt that indeed she was now very wise and so she gave Adam some of the fruit, and he ate it.

Then they sewed fig leaves together to cover themselves as it was now the cool part of the day, and, as they did, they

'Eve gave it to me,' Adam replied.

And the Lord God said to the woman: 'What is this you have done?'

'The serpent tempted me,' Eve told the Lord God, 'and I ate.'

The Lord God was very angry at the serpent and placed a curse on him: thereafter the serpent would have to crawl through life on his belly. Then the Lord God turned to Eve and told her that she would, from this time forth, be ruled by her husband and know great sorrow from her children. Then He told Adam he would have to work the land from whence he came to get his own food. Then the Lord God drove them both from the Garden of Eden. He placed at

heard the voice of the Lord calling to them, but, because they knew they had done wrong, they tried to hide from Him.

'Where are you?' the Lord God called.

And Adam stayed where he was because *he was ashamed.*

And the Lord God asked Adam, 'Have you eaten the fruit I commanded you *not* to eat?'

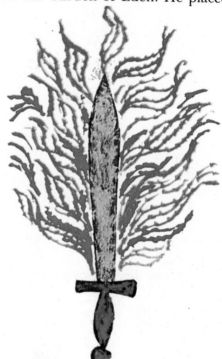

the east of the garden a flaming sword which turned in every direction to guard the Tree of Life so that no man could eat its fruit and therefore live for ever.

•

Cain and Abel

Adam and Eve did as the Lord God said and farmed the land and ate their own food and, as time passed, they had two sons, first Cain and then Abel.

Abel became a shepherd and Cain became a farmer, and, when they both believed the time was right, Cain offered some of his harvest to the Lord and Abel offered to the Lord his fattest and choicest of lambs. The Lord was very pleased with Abel's offering but He did not think Cain's was as good. Cain grew very angry at the Lord!

And God said to him, 'Cain, why are you angry? If you do well with your land I will be pleased with your offering and, if you do not do well, I shall not be pleased.'

But Cain refused to answer, and the anger grew so strong inside him that later, when both he and Abel were back in the fields together, he struck Abel very hard and Abel did not get up!

The Lord God saw this and He called out, 'Cain! What have you done? You have killed your own brother and for that you shall leave this place and never return.'

Cain was frightened that if he were to wander in strange places unknown, someone would try to kill him and the Lord God said to Cain, 'Whosoever slays you shall have seven-fold your sorrow.' Then He placed a mark upon Cain so that anyone finding him would know it was the Lord God's mark and would not kill him.

Cain then went to live in the land of Nod at the east of Eden. He wandered for many years, and then he married and his wife gave birth to a son they called Enoch and Cain built a city named after his son.

The Lord God then gave Eve and Adam another son and they called him Seth. They knew the Lord God now forgave them their past sins so the earth began to grow into the many-peopled place it was to become.

But as time passed and the people multiplied, *so did the evil they could seek.*

•

Genesis 7

Noah and the Ark

At last God saw that man was growing too wicked and He decided He would have to destroy all those He had created: men and beasts and the creeping things and the birds. But there was one old man the Lord thought to spare and his name was Noah. Noah was a just man and so were his three sons – Shem, Ham and Japheth.

God said to Noah, 'Make an ark of yellow gopher wood, with rooms sealed inside and out with pitch. Make it five hundred feet long and eighty-five feet wide and fifty-feet high, with a small window and a door on the top. Then into the ark bring your wife and your sons and your sons' wives and your grandchildren. And of every living thing bring two, a male and a female, and bring as well food for a long journey for all of you, for as soon as your ark is finished and the last animal is on board and the door and the window are shut tight, I will bring a tremendous flood of waters upon the earth and everything that remains shall perish in it!'

•

Genesis 7

The Flood

Noah did as the Lord God told him. He went into the ark with his wife and his sons and his sons' wives and all his grandchildren and all the animals two by two. And, as soon as the last animal was in the ark and the small window and the door were shut tight, the Lord God caused it to rain for forty days and for forty nights and the ark was lifted by the waves above the earth and floated safely on the water.

•

Genesis 8

The Flood Ends

God remembered Noah and every living thing with Noah in the ark and He made the waters go down again and there was no more rain, and Noah and the ark rested safely on the mountains of Ararat.

Then Noah sent out a raven which was not to return until the earth was dry and a dove which *was* to return if the waters were still upon the earth.

The dove came back and so Noah stayed in the ark for another seven days. Then he sent the dove out again. He waited seven days and when the dove did not return he knew the earth was dry and, behold! the earth *was* dry!

Noah left the ark with his wife and his sons and his sons' wives and his grandchildren and every animal, insect and

bird, *everything* that lived left the ark and went out on to the earth to become fruitful and multiply.

And the Lord God told Noah, 'I will not curse the earth again; while the earth remains there will be seed-time and harvest-time and summer and winter and day and night.'

•

Genesis 9

The Rainbow

God blessed Noah and made a special vow that there would not be another flood to destroy the earth and as a token of that vow the Lord God said, 'I set my rainbow in the cloud and it shall come to pass when I bring a cloud over the earth that the rainbow shall be seen in the cloud. I will look upon it and I will remember My vow to you and to every living creature on earth.'

Many years passed and Noah's family grew and went forth to form nations.

•

Genesis 11

The Tower of Babel

At this time all the people on earth spoke one language, and no matter how far they travelled they could understand each other. But, of course, they had only travelled over a small part of the earth. As they moved eastward they finally grew tired and they settled in a land that they called Shinar. They decided to build a city and a tower in this city the very top of which would reach up to Heaven.

Everyone helped and soon the tower was climbing into the clouds and God came down to see what His children were doing. He was very upset! Heaven was a sacred place and could not be entered by building a tower. If this is what His children did when they understood each other then He would have to scatter the people of Babel all over the earth; changing each one's way of speaking so that they could

21

no longer understand each other. The Lord did just that and the tower was left unfinished and it was called, like the city, Babel.

•

Genesis 12

The Promise to Abram

In one of these distant lands lived Abram and his wife, Sarai, and his brother's son, Lot. Abram was a good man and God had been watching him for many years. God spoke to Abram, making him this promise: that if Abram went where God would lead him, and settle there, God would make that land a great nation.

Abram did as God asked of him and with his family went into the land of Canaan. There he pitched his tent on a mountain, but it had not rained for a long time and the earth was dry and there was no food and Abram knew they would all die so he took his family to Egypt to stay until there was rain once more in Canaan.

Now Sarai was very beautiful and Abram was afraid the Egyptians would kill him if they knew Sarai was his wife so that they could marry her. So he told the Pharaoh who ruled the land that Sarai was his sister. Because all the princes *did* want to marry the beautiful Sarai they treated Abram very well and gave him sheep and oxen and many servants.

Then things began to go badly for the Pharaoh and Pharaoh blamed it on Abram and Sarai, but he let them both leave taking with them all that he had given them.

•

Genesis 13–15

Abram and Lot

When Abram returned to Canaan he was rich in cattle and silver and gold, but things were not the same and Abram quarrelled with Lot and there was trouble as well between the men who tended the cattle for Abram and the men who did the same for Lot.

'Let us not quarrel,' Abram told Lot. 'There is so much land.' Abram held up his hands. 'You take all the land on my left hand and I will take all the land on my right.'

Lot could see that the land on the left was the plain of Jordan, which was green and had water and would be good for his cattle and so he thanked Abram and said Goodbye to his uncle and pitched his own tent near Sodom. But the people of Sodom and its twin city of Gomorrah were wicked people and there was a war in the land. Lot and all he owned were captured, but Abram rescued Lot and his goods and all his followers from the people of Sodom.

Abram Becomes Abraham

Abram was very unhappy because he and Sarai had no children and he was ninety-nine years old and Sarai was nearly as old. One day God spoke to him and said, 'No longer will you be called Abram but Abraham, for you will be the father of many nations. I will give you the land of Canaan. Your wife, Sarai, shall now be called Sarah. I will bless her and she will have a son and become the mother of kings.'

Abraham laughed. 'But we are very old to have a son,' he said.

'It shall happen,' the Lord told him, 'and because you could laugh at the Lord's word you will call your son Isaac which means *"he who will laugh."* '

•

Genesis 18

Abraham and the Lord

In the city of Sodom where Lot remained, the wickedness continued and the Lord spoke to Abraham about it. Abraham was frightened that the Lord would destroy the good people of Sodom with the wicked and Lot would be among them. The Lord told Abraham that if He found in Sodom fifty good people He would spare the entire city.

Abraham was very brave before the Lord and he spoke up. 'If You find only forty-five good people would You destroy the city because there were not fifty?'

The Lord answered: 'I shall spare the city if I find *forty* good people in Sodom.'

Abraham grew braver. 'And if there are only thirty good people?' he asked the Lord.

The Lord was angry but He told Abraham, 'If I find ten good people Sodom will not be destroyed,' and then He left Abraham standing there alone.

•

Genesis 19

Lot's Wife

Lot sat at the gates of Sodom. Two Angels came to him and Lot rose and bowed. Then he invited the Angels to lodge at his house. Before nightfall the men of Sodom came to Lot's house and called to him, 'Where are the men who came to you tonight?'

Lot went out to talk to the angry men. 'Do not be so wicked,' Lot told them. 'I have two beautiful daughters and I shall give them to you but you must not touch these men.'

'Stand back!' said the men and they nearly broke the door down but the Angels pulled Lot back into the house and then they made those who crowded round the door blind so that they could not harm Lot and his family.

'Take all your family out of this place,' they told Lot, 'for we are here to destroy it because it has become so evil and the people so wicked, but you are not.'

The next morning the Angels and Lot and his family rose before sunrise and the Angels led Lot and his wife and his family to the gates of the city and told Lot, 'Escape for your life, but *never look back.*'

By the time the sun had risen all of Sodom and nearby Gomorrah were burning but Lot and his family were all safe on the hills. Then Lot's wife looked back and lo! she was turned into a pillar of salt!

•

Genesis 24

Rebecca at the Well

As Abraham grew old he became worried that his son, Isaac, would not marry before he died. He asked his oldest and most trusted servant to do him one last great service.

'Go back to my own country and, from

among my people, choose a wife for my son, Isaac, and bring her here.'

'But what if the girl I choose won't come to Canaan with me?' the servant asked.

'If the girl will not come willingly then you shall come back alone, only do not take my son to that land.'

The servant gave his hand to Abraham and he swore to do as his master had asked him.

The next morning the servant took ten of his master's camels and went to Mesopotamia. There he stopped outside the city and made the camels kneel down beside a well, at the time of the evening when the women and young girls went to draw the water.

The servant said to himself. 'When I look up, let there be a young girl to whom I shall say, "Put down your jug that I may have a drink," and she shall offer my camels a drink as well, so I will know she is kind and a good wife for Abraham's son.'

When the servant looked up there was a lovely girl named Rebecca with her water jug on her shoulder. The servant watched her as she went to the well and filled her jug. The servant ran to meet her.

'Please let me have a drink of water from your jug!' he cried.

'Drink, my lord,' Rebecca said, and she gave him the vessel to take as much water as he wished. Then she said, 'I will draw water for your camels as well,' and she kept filling the trough for the camels to drink from until they had had enough.

●

The Servant at Rebecca's House

The servant gave Rebecca a golden earring and two gold bracelets and she was very pleased.

'Whose daughter are you?' the servant asked.

'I am Rebecca, the daughter of Bethuel,' she told him.

'Is there room in your father's house for us to stay for the night?' he asked.

'There is both straw to sleep on and room to lodge in,' she replied.

And Rebecca's brother came to help lead the servant and the camels to their house. They set a fine dinner before him, but he said to Rebecca's father, 'I cannot eat until I tell you why I am here. I am Abraham's servant and I have come to Abraham's country to find a wife for his son, Isaac. I was not sure that a young girl would follow me willingly so today at the well I prayed and Rebecca appeared as if in answer to my prayers and led me here.'

'It must surely be the wish of the Lord's,' said Rebecca's father. 'Take her to your master's son as a wife.'

They called Rebecca and the servant asked her if she would come willingly with him.

'I will,' said Rebecca, and then Rebecca and her handmaidens rode on the camels with the servant back to Canaan.

●

Isaac and Rebecca

Early one evening Isaac was sitting in his fields thinking of many things when he looked up and saw his father's servant coming towards him with ten camels. As the camels came closer Isaac saw Rebecca sitting on the first camel and Rebecca saw the handsome Isaac and knew immediately this was the man she was to marry. Isaac loved Rebecca from the very first moment and he took her back to his home and they were married.

•

The Twins – Esau and Jacob

Rebecca and Isaac lived very happily but many years passed before they had children. Then they had twins. The first to be born was called Esau and his brother, Jacob. Esau had thick red hair and gew to be a cunning hunter, but Jacob was a plain man who did not like to hunt. Isaac loved Esau more than Jacob because he

liked the thought of his son being a hunter and this hurt Rebecca and she loved the younger brother all the more.

One day Jacob was cooking soup when Esau came from the field. He had been without food a long time and was hungry and faint. 'Feed me,' he begged his brother, 'or I shall die of hunger.'

'Sell me your birthright first,' Jacob said, for Esau being the elder was to inherit all his father's wealth.

'I am so hungry I will do it,' Esau said.

Esau swore to Jacob that he could have his birthright for a bowl of soup. *Then Jacob gave Esau the soup and bread* which had cost Esau his birthright.

•

The Deception

When Isaac was very old he became blind. He called Esau to him and said, 'My son.'

'Here I am,' Esau assured him.

'I am old and I am dying. I want to bless you. Go get your bow and go out to the field and kill a deer. Then cook me the tasty meat which I love and I shall bless you.'

Esau immediately did as his father told him. But Rebecca had overheard the conversation and she was worried that her younger son, Jacob, would not be blessed. So she spoke to Jacob.

'Obey me,' she said. 'Go now to the flock and bring me two small kids and I will make a tasty meal for your father with them. He will then bless *you* and not your brother.'

'But my father will feel me and know that I am Jacob because I haven't the full

'Which son are you?' Isaac asked.

'I am Esau. I have done as you asked me.'

'Come near that I may feel you,' Isaac said.

Jacob went near him and Isaac felt him. 'The voice sounds like Jacob's voice but surely it does feel like Esau. Bring the food near me and I shall eat.'

Jacob brought the food to his father and Isaac ate and afterwards he said, 'Come near now and kiss me, my son.'

Jacob came very close and Isaac kissed him and as he did he smelled his robes and he said: 'It *is* Esau, for your robes smell of the fields. I will bless you. God will give you rich lands and good crops and people will serve you and nations bow down to you. You will be lord over your brother and anyone who curses you shall be cursed themselves.'

As soon as Isaac had given his blessing and Jacob had left, Esau returned from his hunting. He also made a tasty meal for his father and brought it to him.

'Who are you?' his father asked.

'I am Esau, father.'

Isaac trembled. 'Where is your brother who said he was you and whom I have already blessed as you?'

Esau cried bitterly when he heard these words. 'Bless me, too, father!'

Isaac said, 'I cannot go against my word. I have made him your lord and given him servants and your fields.'

Esau hated Jacob then, and vowed he would kill him after his father's death! Rebecca heard of Esau's vow and she called Jacob to her and told him to go to his uncle Laban's home in Haran and stay there until Esau's anger was gone.

growth of hair that Esau has, and he will curse me instead of blessing me because I have lied to him.'

'Obey me,' his mother said. 'It will be my curse then, not yours.'

Jacob got the two small kids and his mother made a tasty meal of them. Then she took Esau's robes and put them on Jacob and put the skins of the kids around his neck so his hair would seem longer to the touch and she gave Jacob the food and he went with it to his father.

'My father,' he said.

•

Jacob Leaves

Rebecca told Isaac that she was unhappy because Jacob had not married a girl from their own country of Haran, and so Isaac called Jacob to him and told him to travel to his mother's house and marry one of his fair cousins. And he blessed Jacob again and sent him away. And so Jacob was free of Esau's anger.

•

Jacob's Dream

Jacob set out on his journey and travelled until the sun had set. Then he took a stone for his pillow and lay down to sleep. He dreamed there was a ladder set up on earth and the top of it reached into Heaven. There were Angels of God going up and down it and the Lord Himself stood at the very top and said in His God's voice, 'I am *the Lord*. The land where you sleep I give to you. I am with you and will keep you safe.'

Jacob woke and he was very frightened. He looked around him and thought *what a dreadful place this is*. He took the stone he had used for a pillow and let it mark the place and he called the place Beth-el.

Jacob said, 'If God will be with me so that I can come again in peace to my father's house, then shall the Lord be my God, and the stone which marks this place shall mark a House of God.'

•

Rachel

Jacob continued his journey and finally came to a new land. He saw a well in a field and three flocks of sheep lying by it.

'My brothers, where are you from?' Jacob asked the shepherds.

'We are from Haran,' they said.

'Do you know my uncle, Laban?' he asked them.

They said, 'We know him.'

'Is he well?' Jacob asked.

'Yes,' they replied, 'but ask his daughter, Rachel, yourself because she is coming with the sheep.'

Rachel ran to tell her father about her cousin's arrival and Laban returned with her. When he saw Jacob, he embraced him and brought him back to his house and asked Jacob to remain with him, and work for him until his brother's anger was gone.

'But I must pay you,' Leban said. 'How much shall that be?'

Now Leban had two daughters and Rachel was the younger. She had an older sister named Leah. Leah was gentle and good but not as beautiful as Rachel. Jacob had loved Rachel from the moment he saw her and so he said, 'I will serve you seven years for your daughter Rachel's hand in marriage.'

Jacob did serve seven years for Rachel and they seemed to him but a few days because he loved Rachel so dearly.

The Wedding

At the end of the seven years Jacob came to Laban and said, 'I have served you well for seven years. Now my time is up. Give me my wife so that I may leave.'

Laban made a great wedding feast, but that evening in the darkness, Laban brought Leah to Jacob and Jacob, thinking she was Rachel, married her. When Jacob found that he had married Leah he went to Laban.

'What have you done?' he said. 'Didn't I serve you for Rachel? Why have you done this to me?'

'In our country it must be this way, because the youngest cannot marry before the first-born and no one has asked for Leah's hand all these seven years. But if you will promise to serve me another seven years I will give you Rachel for a wife, too.'

So Jacob worked for seven more years and took Rachel as his wife, also, for it was the custom in that time for a man to have more than one wife. Jacob loved Rachel more than Leah but Leah gave Jacob many sons. Then Rachel, too, had a son and she called her son Joseph.

Jacob Steals Away from Haran

It was now twenty years since Jacob had come to claim Rachel for his wife and he was very rich. Rachel's brothers were jealous of him and one day Jacob heard them saying, 'Jacob has taken away all the

31

wealth that would be ours.'

Jacob called Leah and Rachel to him. 'God has spoken to me and told me to return to the land of my father, but you are my wives. I must ask you first if we should leave the land of your father,' he said.

'Our father looks at us as strangers,' said Rachel.

'He sold us and used our money and left us without inheritance,' Leah said.

'Whatever God has told you to do, do and we will go with you,' they both said.

So Jacob put all his children and his wives on camels and took with them all his cattle and his belongings and stole away when Laban was in the fields. He fled from Haran over the river towards the mountains.

Jacob is Followed

Laban was in the fields for three days and when he came back and found that Jacob had fled he was very angry. He took his sons and followed Jacob until a week later he overtook him on Mount Gilead.

But God spoke to Laban and warned him not to harm Jacob.

Jacob had pitched his tent on the mountain-side and Laban and his brothers pitched their tents close by. Then Laban spoke to Jacob: 'Why did you steal away without telling me, taking my daughters and my grandchildren with you? I could strike you but the Lord God spoke to me saying that I can do you no harm, yet why have you stolen my goods?'

'I have stolen nothing of yours. Search my followers and my camels and if you find anything of yours then kill that person who stole it!' Jacob said.

But Jacob did not know that Rachel *had* stolen some statues of her father's and hid them under her camel's saddle and was sitting on them! When Laban came close to her she said, 'I am sorry, my lord, but I cannot rise for I am ill.'

Jacob grew angry because Laban wanted to search his own daughters! 'You have searched my belongings,' he said, 'and found nothing! For fourteen years I served you for your two daughters and six more years for your cattle. You have changed my wages ten times and had you not heard God's word you would have sent me away – empty-handed. God saw my suffering and He told you not to harm me, otherwise you would have killed me and taken back my wives and my cattle.'

Laban said, 'I could do you no harm. I swear it!'

Jacob then took a stone and set it in the ground and told his men to gather more stones and they made a great pile of stones and Laban said, 'I will not pass over this pile of stones to harm you and you shall not pass over them to harm me.'

Then they ate on the stone pile and in the morning Leban rose and kissed his grandchildren and daughters and blessed them and returned to his own land.

•

Joseph and his Brothers

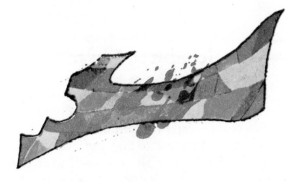

Rachel gave birth to another son whom she and Jacob named Benjamin. Then Rachel died. Joseph grew to be a handsome boy, who loved his baby brother, Benjamin. Every day he would go to the fields with his brothers and feed the sheep. Jacob loved Joseph more than all his sons and made him a coat of many colours. When his brothers saw the beautiful coat they became jealous.

One day, while feeding the flock, Joseph told his brothers, 'I had a dream and in this dream I was tying together a bundle of corn and it stood straight up! And you were all doing the same thing and your bundles of corn also stood up – but they bowed to mine.'

His brothers became even more jealous because Joseph dreamed they would bow to him as if he were their king, and they sent him away from them. Joseph went to his father who told him to go after his brothers. Joseph did, but he could not find them and became lost. An old man found him wandering alone in the fields.

'What are you looking for?' the old man asked.

'My brothers.'

'Oh, they have left and gone to Dotham.'

So Joseph went after his brothers and found them in Dotham. When they saw Joseph their first thoughts were to kill him.

One of his brothers said, 'We can kill him and throw him into a pit and say a wild animal ate him up and then we shall see what happens to his beautiful dreams!'

But his older brother, Reuben, was a gentler sort. 'Let us not kill him,' he said. 'Throw him into a pit if you must but do not harm him.' He said this because he was planning to save Joseph and bring him home to his father again.

Joseph was taken captive by his brothers and they took away his coat of many colours and threw him into a pit that had no water. Then they settled down to eat their evening meal but, as they did so, a band of Ishmaelites came along with their camels loaded with spices they were taking to Egypt.

One of the brothers then had an idea. Why not sell Joesph to the Ishmaelites and make some money as well as rid themselves of him? They all agreed and they lifted the young Joseph out of the pit and sold him for twenty pieces of silver. Their kindly brother Reuben had gone off to get some food for Joseph but when he returned, Joseph was gone!

Then the brothers took the coat of many colours and killed a small animal and dipped the coat into the animal's blood. They brought the coat back to Jacob, who mourned for his son so much that no one, not even the baby, Benjamin, could console him.

And Joseph in the meantime had been taken into Egypt and sold to Pharaoh's captain of the guard.

•

Joseph in Egypt

The Butler and the Baker

Joseph worked hard for his master, Potiphar, the captain of the Pharaoh's guards, in Egypt. Potiphar made him overseer of his estate and put everything in his hands. Joseph was good and the Lord was with him, and Potiphar could see that.

One day Joseph, who had grown to be a handsome young man, was left alone in the house with his master's wife, who had fallen in love with him. She begged Joseph to love her, too. But Joseph told her that he could never love her because it would be a sin and because his master trusted him.

Potiphar's wife was furious! She went to Potiphar and lied to him and told him Joseph had said terrible things to her and Potiphar could do nothing else but send Joseph to prison.

But the Lord was with Joseph and showed him mercy, and the keeper of the prison liked Joseph and was good to him and let him be in charge of many other prisoners, and Joseph was good to them.

●

While Joseph was in prison both the Pharaoh's chief butler and the Pharaoh's chief baker were sent there for displeasing the Pharaoh and they, too, were placed in Joseph's care.

Both of them dreamed a dream in the same night and when Joseph came to them in the morning they looked very sad.

'Why do you look so sad today?' Joseph asked.

'We each dreamed a dream and do not know what the dream means,' they told him.

'Tell me the dreams,' he said.

So the chief butler told his dream to Joseph. 'In my dream there was a vine and in the vine were three branches and there were blossoms and clusters of grapes, and the Pharaoh's cup was in my hand. I took the grapes and pressed them, into the Pharaoh's cup and gave it to the Pharaoh.'

'Ah, well,' said Joseph. 'The three branches were three days. In three days the Pharaoh will make you once again the chief butler. I ask you to remember my kindness to you and mention it to the Pharaoh so that I may be released from here.'

Then the chief baker, pleased with what Joseph had said about the chief butler's dream, told him his own. 'I also was in my dreams and I had three white baskets on my head and in the top basket were the Pharaoh's sweets and the birds ate all of them up so that I had none when I reached the Pharaoh.'

Joseph looked sadly at the chief baker. 'Your three baskets are three days as well,

and they went to the nearby meadow and they ate up the seven fat cows. The dream woke the Pharaoh. Finally he fell back to sleep again but he dreamed another dream! This time seven ears of corn came up as one stalk. They were strong and sweet and then seven ears of corn came up but they were shrivelled and frail and the seven shrivelled ears of corn ate up the seven strong and sweet ears of corn.

The Pharaoh woke up again and this time he could not go back to sleep because he was very disturbed. He sent for all the magicians in Egypt but they could not tell him what the dream meant. Then he sent for all the wise men of the land, but they could not tell him what his dream meant, either. The Pharaoh was very unhappy; then the chief butler remembered Joseph.

'Once,' he told the Pharaoh, 'when you were angry with me you put me in prison with the chief baker. One night we each had a dream and there was with us a young man, a Hebrew, who was a servant to the captain of the guards and we told him our dreams and he told us what they meant and it happened just as he said!'

The Pharaoh sent for Joseph. 'I have had two dreams,' he told Joseph, 'and my magicians and my wise men cannot tell me what they mean, but my chief butler tells me that you could tell me the meaning.'

'If there is a meaning God will give it to the Pharaoh,' Joseph said.

And so Pharaoh told Joseph his two dreams and Joseph listened very atten-

but in three days the Pharaoh will hang you from a tree and there will be birds on the branches.'

In three days the chief butler was released and the baker was hanged as Joseph had said.

Still, the chief butler did not tell the Pharaoh of Joseph's kindness to him.

•

Genesis 41

The Pharaoh's Dream

Two full years passed and Joseph was still in prison. But the Pharaoh now had a dream that he stood by the river and seven fat cows came out of the water to feed in the nearby meadow and then seven scrawny cows came out of the water

he gave him fine linen robes to wear and placed a golden chain around his neck. He bade him ride in his second finest chariot, and the people bowed before him as Pharaoh made him ruler over all the land of Egypt and only second in power to the Pharaoh himself.

Then he gave Joseph the beautiful Asenath, who was the daughter of the Priest of On, to be his wife.

•

Genesis 41

The Seven Years of Plenty Pass

There were, as Joseph said there would be, seven years of plenty and he gathered up all the food he could store and kept it in the cities and near the fields. There was so much food that there was almost no place left to store it.

Joseph's wife, the beautiful Asenath, gave birth to two sons. They called the elder Manasseh and the younger Ephraim.

Then the seven years of plenty ended and the seven years of hunger began. The people cried to Pharaoh for bread and Pharaoh told them, 'Go to Joseph and do as he says.'

Joseph opened the storehouses and gave the Egyptians food. There was enough to send to other lands because the famine had spread, and people from other countries came to Egypt to pay homage to Joseph and buy the food he had stored.

•

tively. When the Pharaoh was finished he said, 'The two dreams are really one. God has shown Pharaoh what He is about to do. The seven good cows and the seven good ears of corn are seven years. The seven scrawny cows that come after are also seven years and the seven shrivelled ears of corn will be seven years of hunger in your land. God is showing Pharaoh that you will have seven years of plenty throughout the whole land of Egypt and then seven years of hunger when all the plenty shall be forgotten. The dream was sent to Pharaoh twice because it will happen soon. Therefore, Pharaoh must find a wise man to look over the crops and appoint officers who will take a fifth of the fat crop during the seven years of plenty so that there will be enough food for the seven years of hunger.'

The Pharaoh said, 'Your plan is wise, Joseph, and you are a wise man. I will place *you* in charge of the land and see that this is done.'

And the Pharaoh took the ring from his hand and put it on Joseph's hand and

Joseph's Brothers Go to Egypt

The famine reached the land of Canaan where Joseph's father, Jacob, and Joseph's brothers still lived. Jacob heard there was corn and food in Egypt, and so, keeping Benjamin by his side, he told his sons to go to Egypt and buy food for all of them. They set off as their father asked.

Joseph was lord of the land and very powerful and anyone who wanted food had to come to him first. It had been so many years since the brothers had seen Joseph that they no longer knew who he was, but when they came before him and bowed down to him Joseph recognized them.

'Where are you from?' he asked.

'The land of Canaan,' they said, still on their knees.

'You are spies!' he told them.

'Oh, no, my lord! We have come only to buy food!'

'I do not believe you.'

'But it is so, my lord. We are twelve brothers, the sons of Jacob in the land of Canaan. Our youngest brother is with our father and another brother is dead.'

'I still do not believe you, but I will give you the chance to prove that what you say is true. All except one of you will be held in prison and that one will travel to Canaan and bring back with him your youngest brother.'

But the brothers could not agree on which one should go because they did not trust each other. So Joseph placed them under guard for three days and at the end of that time he came to them.

'If you do not trust each other, how can I trust you?' he said. Then he took his brother, Simeon, and tied him up before their eyes. Then he told them, 'Go. I will keep this brother here until you bring me back your youngest brother.'

Joseph told his men to fill his brothers' sacks with corn and he placed the money they gave him back into the sacks without their knowing it. Then they loaded their donkey and left Simeon and Egypt.

●

The Brothers Return to Canaan

When the brothers reached Canaan they opened their sacks and found the money. They were very frightened of what the lord of Egypt might do if he thought they had not paid for their food. They then went to Jacob and told him, 'There is a man who is lord over all of Egypt and he took us for spies. We told him we were only twelve brothers, the sons of Jacob, and that Benjamin, still being a child, was with you and that another brother was dead. But he still did not believe us and he tied Simeon up before our eyes and sent us on our way with corn and food in all our sacks, but he told us we must bring Benjamin back to him so that he would know we had not lied. Only then would he release Simeon.'

'And when we emptied our sacks,' another brother added, 'we found the same money we had paid for the corn and now we are frightened.'

'How could this hapen?' Jacob cried. 'First I lose Rachel's son, Joseph. Now Simeon is a prisoner and you ask me to give up Rachel's only other son, Benjamin. I cannot do it. This man may kill you all!'

Reuben beseeched his father, 'I saw a kindness in this man's eyes. When he sees Benjamin he will know we tell the truth and return Simeon to our side.'

'No!' Jacob said. 'I shall not let you take Benjamin. Joseph, his only true brother, is dead and he is all that is left to me of Rachel.'

And Jacob would talk of it no more, though he was saddened that Simeon was a prisoner in a foreign land.

•

Genesis 43

Jacob Sends Benjamin

But soon all the food the brothers had brought back from Egypt was gone and

their wives and children and servants were starving and they went to speak to Jacob again.

'Go to Egypt and buy food,' he told them finally.

'But this man said we could not return without Benjamin. If you will send Benjamin with us we will go, otherwise he may kill us all!'

But Jacob still did not want Benjamin to leave Canaan.

'If you do not let him go, all of us will die of hunger; your sons and their wives and your grandchildren.'

It was very difficult for Jacob but he knew his sons were right, so he said, 'Bring this man a present and double the money so that he will know you intended to pay last time and it was a mistake that the money was returned in your sacks.' Then he looked at Benjamin and held him close. 'May God Almighty see all of you return safely.' Then he kissed Benjamin and sent him with his brothers to Egypt.

•

Genesis 43

Benjamin and Joseph

The brothers arrived in Egypt and went at once to see Joseph. When Joseph saw Benjamin, he had the brothers brought to his house. The brothers were afraid because they thought Joseph would take them as slaves and keep their donkeys, and all because of the money that had been found the previous time in their sacks!

As they neared Joseph's house they said to Joseph's steward, 'Oh, sir, the first time we only came to buy food and when we arrived in Canaan and opened our sacks all our money had been returned. We have brought it back to your lord again with more money for more food. We do not know who put that money in our sacks!'

'Fear not,' the steward told them. 'Your God gave you the money you found. I received your money.'

Then he brought Simeon out to them and Simeon was well and so they went with the steward into Joseph's house and the man told them that they were to eat there. When Joseph came home they all bowed to him again and gave him their presents.

'How are you?' he asked. 'And is the old man, your father, alive?'

'We are well but hungry and our father is still alive and in good health,' and they bowed again to Joseph.

Then Joseph saw Benjamin and he said softly, 'Is that your youngest brother?'

'Yes, my lord.'

Joseph came close to Benjamin. 'God be with you, child,' he said, gently. Benjamin looked up at Joseph and it struck Joseph how much like their mother the child looked and he felt near to tears because it had been a long time since he had been with his small brother. And he left them and went to his own room and wept with happiness. Then he washed his face and returned to his brothers and told his servants, 'Serve the food!' And when the food was served Benjamin was given five times that of his other brothers.

●

The Silver Drinking Cup

When they had done eating Joseph ordered his servants to fill his brothers' sacks with as much food as they could carry and to return their money again to them in the sacks. 'And,' he went on, 'Put my silver cup in the sack of the youngest along with his money.'

The servants did everything Joseph had ordered.

As soon as the morning was light the brothers were sent away and when they were out of the city Joseph told his steward, 'Follow them and when you

overtake them, say, "You have done evil. One of you has stolen my lord's silver drinking cup".'

The man soon caught up with the brothers. 'You have done evil,' he said to them. 'One of you has stolen my lord's silver drinking cup!'

'How could your lord say such a thing? Didn't we bring back the money we found in our sacks from the last trip? Why should we steal silver or gold from your lord's house?'

'If this is so,' another brother said, 'whoever is found to have this drinking cup will die at your hands and the rest of us will be your lord's slaves!'

But Joseph had told his steward otherwise. 'No,' he said, 'my lord only wants the thief; the rest of you shall be able to go on your way.'

Then each man quickly put his sack on the ground and opened it. The sacks were all searched, starting with the oldest brother, at last, Benjamin's sack was searched and, of course, the silver drinking-cup was found there!

The brothers could not believe it! They went back to Joseph's house and fell down on the ground before him.

'How can we clear ourselves?' his brother, Judah, asked. 'We shall *all* be your slaves as well as the one in whose sack you found the silver cup.'

'No,' said Joseph, 'only he shall remain. The rest of you go in peace to your father.'

•

Judah Pleads for Benjamin

Joseph's half-brother, Judah, came closer to Joseph to beseech him, 'Oh, my lord,' he cried, 'please don't take your anger out on the boy! Our father is an old man and the boy was born when he was already old and the boy's mother and his only true brother are both dead and our father loves him dearly! You asked us to bring the boy to you and we told you the lad could not leave his father, for if he did his father would die! Had we not all been starving we would not be here. But our father said to us before we took this second journey, "My wife, Rachel, had two sons. One is dead. If anything should happen to Benjamin I would die, too", and if we return without the lad he *will* surely die! I beg you! Take me in the lad's place as your slave so that my father shall live!'

Joseph was moved by Judah. He told all his servants to leave the room and then he stood facing his brothers.

'I am your brother, Joseph!' he cried, and his brothers were frightened. 'Come closer,' he told them. Still frightened, they came closer. 'I am truly your brother Joseph whom you sold as a slave, but do not be sad or angry for God sent me here through you so that I could save your lives. There has been famine in the land for two years but there are still five years in which the corn will not grow. Go now to our father and tell him that his son, Joseph, is lord over all Egypt and ask him to join me here with all of you and your wives and your children and I will keep you well fed during the time of hunger!'

'It cannot be Joseph!' his brothers said.

Joseph held Benjamin to him. 'See how much we look alike,' he said.

And even though Joseph wore fine robes and gold rings, his brothers could see that what he said was the truth. Benjamin held on to Joseph's robes and hugged him. Joseph and his brothers talked and the past was soon forgotten.

•

Genesis 46

Jacob Goes to Egypt

Joseph told the Pharaoh about his brothers and his father and the Pharaoh told him to have all his family, including his brothers' wives and children, come to Egypt. When Jacob heard Joseph was alive, he started out to see his son, taking all his family with him. And Joseph, in his beautiful chariot, went to meet his father.

It was a very happy meeting and Joseph told his father to tell the Pharaoh that they were shepherds and his father agreed and then Jacob rode in Joseph's chariot to see the Pharaoh.

•

Jacob Meets the Pharaoh

Joseph brought Jacob before the Pharaoh.

'How old are you?' the Pharaoh asked.

'One hundred and thirty,' Jacob told him. Then he blessed the Pharaoh and the Pharaoh gave Jacob and his family the land of Rameses to tend their sheep and cattle, and Joseph made sure his family all had enough food to eat during all the years of the famine.

•

Jacob's Prophecy

The hunger passed and soon the land was rich again and filled with grain. Jacob was now very old indeed and he knew the time had come when he would die, so he called his twelve sons together.

'I will tell you now,' he said when they were all together, 'what will become of you. From you twelve, the twelve tribes of Israel shall be born. Judah's tribe will be the one that will be the greatest but all of you will be blessed.'

Then Jacob lay back on his bed and closed his eyes for ever and Joseph and all Egypt mourned his father for seventy days. Then he placed his father's fine coffin on his chariot and went back to Canaan. But Joseph returned again to Egypt and he forgave his brothers for the

evil thing they had done when he was a boy.

EXODUS

Exodus 1–2

The Birth of Moses

Before Jacob died, God gave him the name of Israel. Therefore, all his children and his grandchildren and all the children after them were called the children of Israel.

It was many years since Joseph and his sons had lived and there was a new Pharaoh in Egypt who did not know the wonderful things Joseph had done. The children of Israel were strong and wise and the new Pharaoh feared they would rise and fight against the Egyptians and overcome them. He therefore made them slaves and made them build great cities for him and worked them very hard. But the harder the Pharaoh made them work the stronger the children of Israel became.

The Pharaoh became angrier still and he spoke to the people and said, 'If a Hebrew child [for so also were called the children of Israel] is born, and it is a son, the nurse shall kill it; but if it is a daughter, it may live.'

But the nurses would not kill the baby boys. The Pharaoh grew angrier yet and he spoke to the nurses, 'Why have you not done as I commanded?'

'Oh, Pharaoh,' the nurses replied, 'the Hebrew women are not like Egyptian women. They have no need for nurses when they have their children, and so how can we tell if a Hebrew child, son or daughter, has been born at all?'

The Pharaoh then spoke to the children of Israel himself. 'Every son you have,' he told them, 'must be thrown into the river! Only your daughters may live.'

But one of the children of Israel had a son and he was so good and beautiful that his mother could not do as the Pharaoh commanded. She took a small basket made of bulrushes and put the baby into it and brought it down to the river's bank and hid it safely in the tall green grass that grew by the sides of the river.

●

'Yes,' said the princess, still holding the beautiful child.

The little girl ran to get her mother and when they returned the princess said to her, 'Take this baby and nurse it for me and I shall pay you for it.'

So the mother took her own child from the princess and took great care of him. And when he was old enough she brought him back to the princess who named him Moses because that meant 'saved,' and she had saved Moses from being drowned.

●

Exodus 2

Moses at the Well

When Moses had grown into a young man, he came upon an Egyptian striking a Hebrew. Moses looked behind him and thought he was quite alone so he killed the Egyptian and then hid him in the sand. The next day he went walking again and this time he saw a Hebrew striking another Hebrew!

'Why are you hitting your own brother?' Moses asked the guilty one.

'Why should you ask that, when you have killed an Egyptian?' the man asked Moses.

Moses knew then that what he had done had been seen and that soon the Pharaoh would find out as well, and so he ran away and kept on going until he reached the land of Midian and here by a well he finally rested.

Now the priest of Midian had seven daughters and they came to draw water from the well. As they did, some neighbouring shepherds frightened them and would not let them near. Moses stood up

Exodus 2

Pharaoh's Daughter Finds Moses

Very soon after, the Pharaoh's daughter came down to the river with her hand-maidens to wash herself and when she saw the basket in the tall grass she sent them to bring it to her.

The Pharaoh's daughter picked up the baby and saw how beautiful it was. She was very sad because she knew it was a Hebrew child and a boy. But the baby's sister had been watching her brother in the basket all the time and drew close to the Pharaoh's daughter.

'Shall I find a nurse from among the Hebrew women?' she asked the princess.

and the shepherds, fearing Moses, left. Moses helped the women water their father's sheep. When they returned to their father he asked, 'How is it you have finished your work so quickly today?'

'There was an Egyptian who helped us water the flock,' they told him.

'Where is this man and why did you not invite him to share our food?' the father asked, and sent them to get Moses.

Moses came to live with the priest and his daughters and fell in love with the one called Zipporah. They had a son and Moses called him Gershon which means 'a stranger there,' because Moses had been a stranger in this land.

●

Exodus 3–4

God Speaks to Moses

Moses tended the sheep for his father-in-law, the priest of Midian. One day while he led the flock, a nearby bush caught fire and there were great flames but when the fire was out, the bush was not burnt. Moses went closer to see why the bush had not burnt.

'Moses, Moses!' It was the voice of God.

'Here I am,' Moses replied.

'Do not come any closer until you take off your shoes, for the ground on which you are standing is holy ground.'

Moses took of his shoes and came closer to the bush.

'I have seen how your people have suffered,' God told him. 'I have heard them cry and I am going to bring them out of Egypt into a beautiful land of milk and honey. You are to go to Pharaoh and lead my people, the children of Israel, out of Egypt.'

But Moses asked the Lord, 'How can I?'

'I will be with you,' God told him, 'and, when you have done as I say, you shall say your prayers to *Me* upon this mountain.'

'When I tell the children of Israel "the God of your fathers has sent me," they will ask your name. What shall I say to them?'

'Say: "The Lord God of your Fathers, the God of Abraham, the God of Isaac and the God of Jacob has sent me. His name is Jehovah, and He appeared before me and told me how the children of Israel have suffered in Egypt and commanded me to lead you into another land". They will listen to you. Then you shall go with the older men to the Pharaoh and tell him: "The Lord God of the Hebrews has called us and we beg you to grant us three days to travel to His mountain in the wilderness and say prayers to Him." I am sure the Pharaoh will not let you go but I will perform wonders and after that he will let you go, and when he does you shall not go empty-handed.'

'They won't believe me,' Moses said. 'They shall say, "The Lord has not appeared to you".'

'What is it that you have in your hand?' the Lord asked.

'A rod.'

'Throw it on the ground.'

Moses did and the rod became a snake! 'Now take the serpent by the tail,' the Lord commanded. Moses did and the snake became a rod again! 'Now,' the Lord continued, 'put you hand against your chest.' Moses did this and, when he took it away, it was white as snow and not like his hand at all. 'Now put your hand against your chest again.' Moses did and this time when he took it away, it was once more his own hand.

'If they do not believe you or listen to you by the first sign, then they should believe the second sign, but if they do not, then you shall take water from the river and pour it on the dry land and it will become blood.'

But Moses was still not sure. 'O my Lord. I am not a good speaker,' he apologized.

'Who has made man's mouth? Was it not I? Go. I will be your voice.'

'I beg You send someone else,' Moses said.

God became angry with Moses and would listen no longer. 'Your brother, Aaron, speaks well and he will come to meet you. I will show both of you what to do. Now! Take the rod in your hand and go!'

•

Exodus 4

Moses Goes Back to Egypt

Moses went home and asked his father-in-law to let him return to Egypt to see if his own family might still be alive.

'Go in peace,' his father-in-law said.

Then God, pleased with Moses, told him he could return to Egypt without fear, as all the men who knew about the

Egyptian he had killed were now dead. Then God spoke to Moses' brother, Aaron. 'Go into the wilderness to meet Moses,' He said. Aaron went and he and Moses met at the Mountain of God. Moses told Aaron all that the Lord had told him and all the signs He asked him to make.

Moses and Aaron then went back to Egypt and gathered together all the Hebrew elders and Aaron spoke all the words to them that God had spoken to Moses and he did all the signs for the people to see.

The people believed Aaron and Moses and, when they heard that the Lord had seen their suffering and had sent Moses to lead them out of Egypt, they bowed their heads and gave thanks.

•

Exodus 5

The Cruel Pharaoh

Moses and Aaron went into the Pharaoh's palace. 'The Lord God has spoken to us,' they said. 'He has said that you must let our people go so that they may hold a feast in His honour in the wilderness.'

'Who is this Lord, that I, Pharaoh of all Egypt, should obey His voice? I will not do as He says,' the Pharaoh said, angrily.

'Let us go, we beg you, or else our Lord will be angry and cause us death and sickness.'

But the Pharaoh made the Hebrews work even harder. 'You shall no longer give the people straw to make the bricks as you have so kindly done in the past,' he told his officers. 'Let them gather straw for themselves. But they shall have to make the same number of bricks. The men will have no time then to listen to empty talk of a God.'

The Pharaoh's officers did as the Pharaoh said and they stood over the children of Israel with whips, as if they were animals. The children of Israel then went to the Pharaoh.

'Why do you beat us when we are working as hard as we can?' they cried.

'Go from my presence!' the Pharaoh replied. 'You will not be idle a minute to think of your God!'

The Hebrews left the Pharaoh's presence and they met Moses and Aaron. 'You have made the Pharaoh hate us even more!' they shouted. 'Next he will kill us all!'

•

Exodus 6

God Renews His Promise

Moses spoke to the Lord again. 'Since I spoke to the Pharaoh as You told me to do,' Moses said, 'the Pharaoh has been even crueller to the children of Israel and You have let this happen!'

Then the Lord said to Moses: 'Now you shall see what I will do to the Phar-

aoh so that he will make our people leave Egypt. You speak to the children of Israel and tell them the Lord God will free them from slavery and make them His people and will lead them to the Promised Land.'

Moses repeated the Lord's words to the children of Israel, but they would not listen.

God spoke to Moses again: 'Go to the Pharaoh again and let Aaron tell him to let the children of Israel leave his land.'

'If my own people wil not listen to me, why should the Pharaoh?' Moses asked the Lord.

The Lord God replied, 'You will do as I say. Aaron shall speak to the Pharaoh and tell him to send the children of Israel out of his land. If the Pharaoh does not do as I command, then I shall send My own armies into Egypt and his people shall suffer, but the children of Israel will remain safe to leave his land.'

The Magic Rods

Moses and Aaron went to the Pharaoh and said what the Lord had commanded. Then Aaron threw down his rod and it became a snake!

The Pharaoh called his wise men and his magicians. They all threw down their rods and the rods became snakes; but Aaron's rod, which was the largest snake, consumed the others until there were none but Aaron's.

But the Pharaoh still would not do as the Lord God of the Hebrews demanded.

THE TEN PLAGUES

Exodus 7

One: The Plague Upon the River

Then the Lord spoke to Moses: 'Tell Aaron,' He said, 'to take your rod and wave it over the water of Egypt, over their streams and their ponds, and even their pools of water, and the water will become blood.'

Moses and Aaron did as the Lord God comanded with Pharaoh and all his servants watching and all the water *did* become blood! The fish that were in the rivers died and the Egyptians could not drink the water. The Pharaoh's wise men and magicians could do nothing to stop this terrible plague but the Pharaoh went back to his palace and still refused to let the children of Israel go.

The Egyptians dug around the river to find water to drink but for seven days there was none.

Exodus 8

Two: The Plague of the Frogs

After the seven days the Lord spoke again to Moses. 'Go to Pharaoh,' He told Moses, 'and say to him, "Let my people go, for if you do not, the Lord God will send a plague of frogs which shall go into your houses and your bedrooms and on to your beds, and into the houses of all the people of Egypt and even into their ovens." Tell Aaron to wave your rod over the streams and it shall happen as I say.'

Moses went to the Pharaoh and he still refused to let the children of Israel leave Egypt. Aaron then took the rod and waved it over all the rivers and the frogs came up and on to the land. Pharaoh called Moses to him. 'Entreat your Lord to take away the frogs and I will let your people go,' he said.

'When shall I do this?' Moses asked.

'Tomorrow,' the Pharaoh replied.

'It shall be done as you say so that you will see that there is no one like the Lord our God. The frogs will disappear from the land and return to the rivers.'

Moses prayed to the Lord and the Lord made the frogs disappear, but when the Pharaoh saw the frogs were gone he changed his mind and still refused to let the children of Israel go.

Three: The Plague of the Lice

Then the Lord told Moses: 'Tell Aaron to take your rod and strike the earth with it and then the dust will become lice and the lice will spread all over Egypt.'

Aaron did this and it was as the Lord said.

The magicians could not make the lice disappear and they said to the Pharaoh, 'This is the finger of God,' but the Pharaoh still refused to let the children of Israel go.

Exodus 8

Four: The Plague of the Flies

The Lord then told Moses to rise early in the morning and meet the Pharaoh when he would be standing by the river. 'Tell him,' God said, 'that I will send swarms of flies over all Egyptian homes but in the homes of the children of Israel there shall be no flies so he shall know *I am the Lord.*'

And the Lord did as He said He would.

Pharaoh called Moses to him. 'I will let you go so that you can pray to your Lord in the wilderness, but you shall not go too far away.'

'I will ask the Lord to make the flies disappear but, Pharaoh, you must not lie to us again and not let our people go.'

Moses left the Pharaoh and prayed to the Lord and the Lord made all the flies disappear. But the Pharaoh went back on his word and still did not let the children of Israel go.

•

Six: The Plague of the Boils

Now the Lord God told Moses and Aaron, 'Take handfuls of ashes from a furnace and throw them towards heaven when the Pharaoh is watching. The ashes shall become fine dust throughout Egypt and all whom the dust shall touch, man or animal, shall break out in painful boils.'

Moses and Aaron did as the Lord said and even the magicians could not use their magic because they were in such pain from the boils, but the Pharaoh still refused to let the children of Israel leave!

•

Five: The Plague of the Cattle

Moses went to the Pharaoh again. 'My Lord says you shall let His people go. He will give you until tomorrow and if you still refuse there shall be another terrible plague and all your horses and donkeys and camels and sheep and oxen and cattle shall die, but nothing that belongs to the children of Israel shall die.'

The Pharaoh still would not do as Moses asked and so the next day all the cattle and horses and oxen and sheep and camels of the Egyptians died, but the ones that belonged to the children of Israel still lived.

Still Pharaoh refused to let the people go!

•

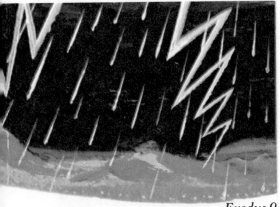

Exodus 9

Seven: The Plague of Hail and Fire

'Tomorrow,' the Lord told the Pharaoh through Moses and Aaron, 'about this time I will make it hail and rain as it never has before in Egypt. Therefore, gather all that you have in your fields and bring it home, for every man who is still in the fields and all things growing on them shall die.'

Some Egyptians now feared the word of the Lord and brought their servants and their cattle into their houses, but those who did not believe the word of the Lord left their servants and cattle in the fields and the next day God made Moses raise his rod towards the sky and it began to thunder and hail, and lightning struck the ground. Nothing like it had ever been seen before! And all those in the fields died.

The Pharaoh sent for Moses and Aaron. 'It is enough!' he cried. 'The Lord is just and I am wicked! Pray to the Lord to stop the thunder and the hail and the lightning and I will let your people go!'

Moses prayed to the Lord and the lightning and hail and thunder stopped, but when the Pharaoh saw this he sinned again and still would not let the children of Israel go!

•

Exodus 10

Eight: The Plague of the Locusts

'I have let all these things happen,' the Lord told Moses, 'so that you may tell your son and your son's son what I have done in Egypt and you will know *I am the Lord.* You will now tell the Pharaoh that if he still refuses to let My people go, the next day Egypt shall be covered with locusts and they shall eat everything left to eat.'

Moses and Aaron told the Pharaoh this and Pharaoh's servants begged him to let these people leave Egypt so that Egypt would not be destroyed.

'But,' said the Pharaoh, 'I will not let all your children go. Only your men.'

Then the Lord caused an east wind to blow over the land all that day and all that night, and when it was morning the east wind brought locusts and the locusts covered the land of Egypt and the land was black with them and they ate every plant and all the fruit from the trees. Not one green thing was left.

Pharaoh summoned Moses and Aaron as quickly as he could!

'Forgive me, I beg you! Pray to your Lord to end this terrible plague!'

Moses and Aaron left the Pharaoh and prayed to the Lord and He sent a stronger west wind which blew all the locusts into the sea.

But still the Pharaoh hardened his heart and refused to let the children of Israel go!

•

Exodus 10

Nine: The Plague of Darkness

Then the Lord said to Moses, 'Stretch out your hand towards the heavens so that there will be a darkness over the land of Egypt so thick it will be felt.'

And Moses stretched out his hand towards the heavens and there was a thick darkness throughout the land of Egypt for three days, but the children of Israel had light wherever they lived.

Pharaoh called Moses to him again. 'Your people and your children may go if this darkness is lifted from my land but your cattle and your flocks shall be left behind,' he said.

Moses refused to leave behind one animal and the Pharaoh said to him, 'Leave my presence! Make sure I never see your face again, for if I do I shall have you killed!'

'You have spoken well, O Pharaoh,' Moses replied. 'You shall never see me again.'

•

Exodus 11

Ten: The Plague of the First born

The Lord told Moses, 'I will bring one more plague upon the Pharaoh and upon Egypt. Afterwards he will ask you to leave altogether. Talk to the people, for you are very great in the eyes of Pharaoh's servants and in the eyes of the people.'

So Moses told the people as the Lord had said: 'About midnight I will come among you and all the first-born in the land of Egypt shall die, from the Pharaoh's first-born to the first-born of all the animals in Egypt, but not one child of Israel shall die. You will know then that the Lord has favoured the children of

Israel! All who follow the Pharaoh will soon bow down to me!'

But the Pharaoh still would not let the children of Israel go out of his land.

•

Exodus 12

The Time of the Passover

The Lord then told Moses, 'Tell all the children of Israel that this month shall be the first month of the year for them and on the tenth day of this month they shall take a lamb from their flocks and keep it until the fourteenth day of the month and then, when all are gathered together, kill the lamb. Then you are to take the lamb's blood and make one mark with it on the sides of your front doors and three marks above your front doors. Then roast the lamb and eat it with unleavened bread and bitter herbs. You shall eat until nothing is left for the morning and you shall eat in haste, ready to leave. It is the Lord's passover. For I will pass through the land of Egypt this night and in the morning all the first-born of the Egyptians shall be dead, but where I see blood on a house I shall pass over and the plague shall not touch you, and from this day forth this day shall be a holy day and you shall keep it as a feast to the Lord for ever. You will keep this holy day to remember that on this day I brought your people out of the land of Egypt.'

Moses called together all the older people of the children of Israel and told them as well, 'When you reach the land which the Lord has promised you, you will keep these holy days as long as any child of Israel lives. And when your children ask you, "What do these holy days mean?" you shall say, "They are our sacrifice to the Lord for passing over the houses of the children of Israel when He plagued the Egyptians and led us out of slavery".'

The children of Israel went home and did as the Lord God had told them to do and at midnight He passed through the land, but *over* the houses of the children of Israel, and when Pharaoh woke up during the night there was not one house which belonged to an Egyptian in which someone did not die that night.

Pharaoh then called Aaron and Moses to him. 'Go,' he told them, 'and take your little ones and your flocks and your herds and be gone! And bless me, too!'

So the children of Israel took their bread that was not raised, and tied up their clothes in bundles over their shoulders and took jewels of silver and gold from the Egyptians and left Egypt. Then they travelled from Rameses to Succoth. There were six hundred thousand of them, not including the children, and they travelled on foot with their flocks and their herds of cattle.

That first night of the Passover ended four hundred and thirty years that the children of Israel had been living in slavery in Egypt.

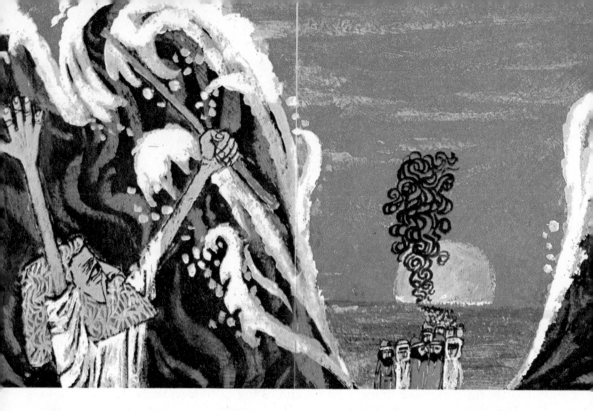

Exodus 13–14

Moses Crosses the Red Sea

The children of Israel continued their journey from Succoth. The Lord led them by day as a pillar of cloud and by night as a pillar of fire, and so they had light both day and night.

Now the Egyptians spoke to the Pharaoh. Without the children of Israel to serve them they had to do their own work, which did not please them. The Pharaoh chose six hundred of the finest chariots in all Egypt and put captains over all of them. Then they followed the children of Israel until they overtook Moses and his followers beside the Red Sea. The children of Israel were very frightened and they said to Moses, 'Why have you led us into the wilderness to die? It would have been better for us to serve the Egyptians.'

'Do not be afraid,' Moses assured them. 'This will be the last time you will see the Egyptians. The Lord will show us the way.'

Then God spoke to Moses: 'Lift up your rod and stretch your hand over the sea. The sea will part in two and in the middle there shall be dry land for the children of Israel to cross to the other side.'

Then the pillar of cloud in which the Lord had led the children of Israel moved until it was behind them and separated the Egyptians from them so that they could not be seen, because although it was a cloud of light for Moses' followers it was a cloud of darkness for Pharaoh's soldiers!

Then Moses stretched out his hand over the sea and the Lord made a strong east wind push the sea back and by morning the sea had parted and the children of Israel crossed over on dry ground. But the Egyptians followed them.

Then the Lord told Moses, 'Now stretch out your hand over the waters and the sea will be one water again,' and Moses did and the waters returned and covered the chariots and the horsemen. *There was not one left!*

Thus the Lord saved the children of Israel.

Exodus 15

The Bitter and the Sweet Waters

The children of Israel travelled on into the wilderness for three days after crossing the Red Sea and they found no water. When they came to a place where there was water they could not drink it because it was bitter and they called this place Marah, which means 'bitter.'

'What shall we drink?' the people asked Moses.

And the Lord showed Moses a tree and when the tree had been thrown into the water the water was sweet and they could drink it.

And the Lord told them, 'If you will listen to *My* voice and carry out *My* commands, you will never have the plagues I brought upon the Egyptians.'

They came next to a place called Elim, where there were twelve wells of sweet water and seventy palm trees, and they camped there.

Exodus 16

The People Find Manna

The children of Israel journeyed into the wilderness and six weeks passed and they now had no food, and they cried to Moses, 'You have brought us into the wilderness to die of hunger!'

But the Lord told Moses, 'I will rain bread from heaven for you and the people shall go out and gather a certain amount each day and on the sixth day they shall prepare what they bring in and it shall be twice as much as they gather daily. In the evening you shall eat meat and in the morning you shall have your fill of bread and you shall know that I am the Lord your God.'

That evening, birds flew over the camp and they ate the meat and in the evening a dew covered the ground and when the dew was gone they saw small white pieces on the ground that they called *manna*, which Moses told them was bread. They gathered the bread. Some took more and some took less but when they measured it they all had the same amount! On the sixth day they gathered twice as much bread and came to Moses and praised what had happened.

'This is what the Lord has said,' he told them. 'Tomorrow you shall rest and not

work. It will be the Holy Sabbath. Take what you gathered today and bake it all so that you will have it to eat tomorrow. For six days you shall gather bread but on the seventh day there will be none.'

But there were some who went out on the seventh day and found none!

•

Exodus 16

The Sabbath

'How long will you refuse to obey what I say?' the Lord asked Moses. 'The Lord has given you on the sixth day enough bread for two days. No man shall go out on the seventh day which is the Sabbath.'

So people rested on the Sabbath and ate the manna which was white and tasted like biscuits made with honey.

•

The Water from the Rock

And the children of Israel travelled on and came next to Rephidim, where they pitched their tents. But there was no water to drink.

'Give us water!' the people shouted at Moses.

And Moses asked the Lord, 'What shall I do? The people are ready to stone me.'

'Go before the people with your rod and let them follow you to the river. There will be the rock of Horeb there and you shall strike it with your rod and water will pour out of it for the people to drink.'

And Moses did as the Lord said and the people had water to drink.

•

Moses on Mount Sinai

The children of Israel travelled on until they came to the wilderness of Sinai. And the Lord called Moses to the mountain.

'You shall obey my voice and keep your agreement with me and then you shall be a chosen people.'

'All that the Lord asks we will do,' the people told Moses.

God was pleased and called Moses again to Mount Sinai. 'I will come in a thick cloud so that the people will hear my words as you do and believe you for ever. Go now and let the people wash their clothes and be ready for the third day, for I shall come down in sight of all the people upon Mount Sinai. The people must be warned that they cannot go up the mountain or touch it. Anyone who does so will be killed. When the trumpet sounds they shall come up to Mount Sinai.'

The morning of the third day there was thunder and lightning and a thick cloud lay upon the montain. A trumpet blasted so loud that all the people trembled.

Moses led the people to the foot of the mountain. Mount Sinai was covered with smoke. The smoke rose up and the whole mountain trembled and shook.

The trumpet grew louder and louder and Moses spoke to God and God answered him. Then the Lord came down upon the top of Mount Sinai and He called Moses up to the top of the mountain and Moses went.

The War with Amalek

While the children of Israel were in Rephidim an army led by a man named Amalek attacked them. Moses spoke to Joshua and told him, 'Choose men to fight Amalek and tomorrow I will stand on top of the hill with the rod of God in my hand.'

Joshua did as Moses asked and went out with the men he had picked to fight Amalek, and Moses, Aaron and Hur went to the top of the hill. There Moses held up his hand and when he did Joshua and his men were winning but when he lowered his hand Amalek moved forward. Moses' hands were heavy and it was difficult for him to keep them in that position and so they took a stone and made him sit on it, and with Aaron on one side and Hur on the other they held up his hands so that by sundown Amalek's army was beaten.

Exodus 20

The Ten Commandments

And then God spoke all these words: 'I am the Lord God who brought you out of the land of Egypt and out of slavery and these are My ten commandments:

1. You shall have no other gods but Me.

2. You shall not make any statues or any likenesses of anything that is in heaven above or on the earth beneath, or in the water under the earth. You shall not bow down to them or serve them, for I am a jealous God who will punish the children of those who hate Me and show mercy to those who love Me and keep My commandments.

3. You shall not take the name of the Lord your God in vain.

4. Remember the Sabbath Day and keep it holy.

5. Honour your father and your mother.

6. You shall not kill.

7. You shall not commit adultery.

8. You shall not steal.

9. You shall not wrongly accuse your neighbour.

10. You shall not envy a neighbour's wife or his servants or his animals or anything that is your neighbour's.

The people heard the thunderings and the sound of the trumpet and saw the lightnings and the mountain smoking and they stood back and they said to Moses, 'You speak to us and we will listen, but we may die if we listen to God!'

'Don't be frightened,' Moses told them. 'God is just testing you so that you will learn to respect Him and won't do wrong.'

The people stood far off but Moses went closer and into the darkness where God was.

●

Exodus 23

The Angel of God

God also told the people, 'You shall have three feasts a year to Me; the feast of the unleavened bread, the feast of the harvest and the feast of the in-gathering when all the harvests have been gathered, and three times a year all your males shall appear before the Lord.

'I shall send an Angel before you to show you the way of the place I have prepared for you. Beware of him and obey him for he will not forgive your sins. But if you do indeed obey him then I will be an enemy to your enemies and a friend to your friends.

'You shall serve the Lord and He shall bless your bread and your water and take sickness away.

'I will not drive out the people of the lands you are going to because the land may grow bare and the animals multiply and turn against you. But little by little I shall drive them out and your families will increase and you will inherit the land.'

●

Exodus 24–31

The Lord's Ark

Moses wrote down all the words of the Lord and the people said, 'All the Lord has said we will do.'

Then God said to Moses, 'Come up to me in the mountain and I will give you tablets of stone with the law and the commandments on them so that you can teach them.'

Moses and his minister, Joshua, went into the mountain of God and when Moses went to the mountain a cloud covered it for six days. Moses went into the cloud and remained on the mountain for forty days and forty nights.

God told Moses, 'The people of Israel shall make Me an Ark of acacia wood. It shall be a chest four feet long, two and a half feet wide and two and a half feet high. It is to be covered with gold inside and out and it shall have gold rings and through these rings shall be passed gold-covered rods of acacia wood so that the Ark may be carried. Inside the Ark shall be placed the laws I gave you.

'Then the people shall make Me a throne of pure gold, four feet long and two feet wide: At each end there shall be the figure of an Angel and the Angels shall stretch their wings upward covering the throne with them. They shall face one another and they shall be looking down and the throne shall be placed on top of the ark.

'Then they shall make a table of acacia wood and cover it with gold and put a gold band around it with gold rings at each corner. And then they shall make a candlestick of pure gold with three branches on either side so that there shall be a place for seven candles.

'Then you will have the people put up a tent lined with fine linen and with blue and purple and scarlet cloth and the ark and the throne shall be kept in here and covered with a curtain of blue and purple and scarlet cloth.

'Every Sabbath twelve loaves of bread shall be placed there to be eaten by the priests. And the people of Israel shall make an altar and set it up before the tent.

'Aaron and his sons shall become My priests. You shall make holy garments for Aaron for glory and beauty: a breast-plate, a shawl, a robe, an embroidered coat, a turban and a belt. The shawl shall be made of gold and blue and purple and scarlet linen. The breastplate shall have chains of pure gold and another gold plate engraved with the words *Holiness to the Lord* shall be put in the front of his turban and worn on his forehead. Aaron must wear this plate at all times and he and his sons shall be made priests.'

And when God had finished talking to Moses upon Mount Sinai He gave him two tablets of the law and the commandments written in the hand of the Lord.

•

Exodus 32

The Golden Calf

When the people saw that Moses was not coming down from the mountain they gathered around Aaron and said to him, 'Make us gods for we do not know what has become of Moses.'

70

Aaron told them to bring all their golden ear-rings from their wives and daughters to him and they did and Aaron melted the gold and made it into a golden calf.

'Let this be your god,' he said. Then he made an altar before it and told the people: 'Tomorrow is a feast day to the Lord, the Golden Calf.'

The people got up early in the morning and brought offerings to the golden calf; then they ate and drank and danced.

God told Moses, 'Go, for your people have sinned and broken one of My commandments!'

And though the Lord was hot with anger, Moses spoke to Him and He relented and did not turn His anger on the people.

●

Exodus 32

The End of the Golden Calf

Moses went down the mountain and carried the two tablets of the laws written in God's hand. When Joshua heard the people's loud voices he said, 'There is war in the camp.'

'Not war,' Moses told him, 'but the sound of singing.'

As soon as Moses came near the camp he saw the calf and the dancing and he grew angry and cast the tablets down and broke them. Then he took the calf they had made and burnt it in the fire and ground it to powder and stirred it into the water and made the people of Israel drink it!

The next day Moses said to the people, 'You have sinned badly. Now I will go up to the Lord. Perhaps I can get Him to forgive you.'

When Moses spoke to the Lord the Lord told him, 'Go, lead the people to the place I have told you. My Angel shall go before you. The time shall come when I shall punish the people for their sin.'

●

commanded, holding the two tablets of stone. God came down in the cloud and stood with him there.

God said, 'I will make a promise. I will do wonders for all your people as have never been done elsewhere before. All your people shall see the work of the Lord. But you must keep all My commandments and worship Me according to My laws.'

Moses stayed with the Lord for forty days and forty nights and he did not eat or drink during this time, and he wrote the ten commandments and the words and the law on the tablets.

When Moses came down from Mount Sinai with the tablets his face was shining so brightly that the children of Israel were afraid to come close to him. Moses put a veil over his face and spoke, telling them what the Lord had said; then he took off the veil and the children of Israel looked upon his shining face.

The children of Israel then made all the things that the Lord had commanded. They raised the tent for the Ark and the Lord covered it with a cloud when they were to rest and removed it when they continued their journey.

Exodus 34–40

A Renewed Promise

God said to Moses, 'Take two tablets of stone like the first and I will write upon these tablets the words that were on them when you broke the tablets. Come up in the morning to Mount Sinai and stand there before Me at the top of the mountain, and you must come alone.'

So Moses cut two tablets of stone like the first and rose early in the morning and went up Mount Sinai as the Lord had

NUMBERS

The Princes of Israel

The Lord spoke to Moses in the wilderness of Sinai and He said: 'Take all the male children of Israel from twenty years of age on, all that are able to fight for Israel, and number them. There shall be twelve tribes from the twelve sons of Israel, and twelve princes, each one named for Israel's sons. They shall be:

The Tribe of Reuben with Elizur as prince.
The tribe of Simeon with Shelumiel as prince.
The tribe of Judah with Nahshon as prince.
The tribe of Issachar with Nethaneel as prince.
The tribe of Zebulun with Eliab as prince.
The tribe of Joseph with Elishama as prince.
The tribe of Manasseh with Gamaliel as prince.
The tribe of Benjamin with Abidan as prince.
The tribe of Dan with Ahiezer as prince.
The tribe of Asher with Pagiel as prince.
The tribe of Gad with Eliasaph as prince.
The tribe of Naphtali with Ahira as prince.

But the Lord asked Moses not to number the tribe of the Levites. Instead they became the guards of the Holy Tent, carrying it with them wherever the children of Israel travelled. They were to pitch it and take it down and any stranger who interfered would be put to death.

•

The Great Cloud

The children of Israel continued on their journey. A cloud covered the Holy Tent during the daytime and a fire burned beside it at night, but they would not move on until the cloud lifted and moved before them even if it remained for two days, or a month, or a year.

Numbers 13

The Twelve Spies

When they had reached Paran, near the land of Canaan, Moses chose twelve men, one from each of the tribes of Israel, to go to the land of Canaan as spies.

'Go up into the mountains,' He told them, 'and look over the land to see what it is like. Find out if the people who live there are weak or strong and how many there are. See whether the earth is rich or not. See if there are trees – and bring back the fruit of the land.'

The twelve spies went out and searched the land ahead of them. They came to a brook and there they cut down a branch with a cluster of grapes on it. As they went on they picked pomegranates and figs. When they returned to Moses and Aaron and the children of Israel they showed them the fruit.

'It is indeed a land of milk and honey,' they said, 'yet the people are strong and the cities are walled and very large. We saw the children of Anak there. To the south are the Amalekites; in the mountains are the Hittites, the Jehusites and the Amorites, and the Canaanites have the land by the sea and along the river Jordan.'

Caleb, who had been one of the twelve spies, said, 'Let us go at once and take possession of the land. We are strong enough!'

But some of the others said, 'We are not able to fight these people! You are wrong. They are stronger than we and the land is a land that eats up the people who live there. All the people are huge. The sons of Anak are giants! We looked like grasshoppers beside them!'

●

Numbers 14

Joshua and Caleb Speak

Then all the people lifted up their voices and cried. They turned against Moses and Aaron. 'Let us choose a new leader and let us return to Egypt!' they shouted.

Caleb and Joshua, who had been two of the twelve spies, spoke to the people. 'The land we went through,' they said, 'is good land. If the Lord is pleased with us and gives it to us it will truly be a land flowing with milk and honey. But do not go against the Lord and do not fear the people of the land. The Lord is with us.'

But the people nearly threw stones at Caleb and Joshua and God grew very angry and spoke to Moses.

'How long will these people do things to make me angry?' He said. 'How long will it be before they believe in Me and the signs I show them? If they continue like this, I will strike them with a plague and disinherit them and make a great nation of *you* alone!'

●

Numbers 17–18

The Twelve Rods

The Lord told Moses, 'Talk to the children of Israel and have each tribe give you a rod and on each of the twelve rods write one man's name. The man's rod which I shall choose shall blossom.'

Moses collected all the rods and placed them before the Lord in the Holy Tent. The next morning the rod of Aaron for the house of Levi had buds and blossoms and almonds on it. Moses brought out all the rods to show the children of Israel and every man took back his own rod, for the Lord had separated Aaron and his brother, Moses, from the rest.

●

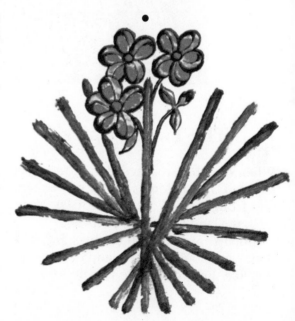

The Water and the Rock

The children of Israel wandered into the desert of Zin. Once again there was no water and God spoke to Moses.

'You and Aaron take the rod and gather the people together. Speak to the rock while the people watch. Soon it shall spout water enough for all the people and their cattle to drink.'

So Moses gathered all the people together before the rock and said to them, 'I shall bring water out of this rock.' Then he raised his hand and struck the rock twice with his rod and the water came flowing out.

•

Numbers 20

King Edom

Moses sent messengers from Kadish to the King of Edom and said to him, 'We the people of Israel are at your borders. Let us pass, I beg you. We will not tramp through your fields or drink from your wells. We will not turn right or left until we have passed the far borders of your country.'

But King Edom would not let them pass.

•

Numbers 20

Aaron Dies

The people went instead to Mount Hor and there on the top of the mountain

Aaron died and his son, Eleazar, put on his priest's robes and came down the mountain with Moses. And when the people heard Aaron had died they mourned him for thirty days.

•

Numbers 21

The Brass Serpent

In order to go around the land of Edom, the children of Israel travelled from Mount Hor by way of the Red Sea. But the people were very discouraged and spoke against the Lord and the Lord sent fierce serpents among the people. The people came to Moses and begged him to ask the Lord to take the serpents away and Moses told them, 'Make a serpent of brass and put it on a pole. Everyone who has been bitten by a serpent shall live if he looks upon it.'

This had been God's command, so when the pole was made those who had been bitten by a serpent looked at the brass serpent and they lived.

•

King Balek Sends Messengers

Time passed and the children of Israel were living in the plains of Moab, on the side of the river Jordan near Jericho. King Balek was a neighbouring king and, knowing what the children of Israel did to the land of Bashan and the land of the Amorites, was frightened that the children of Israel would take over his country as well. Therefore, he sent messengers to King Balaam who was his neighbour and said to him, 'There is a tribe of people that has come from Egypt and soon they will conquer the world if we don't stop them. Join with me to fight them for they are too many and too strong for me.'

King Balaam gave the messengers lodging for the night and told them he would speak to God.

'What men are these to whom you have given lodging?' the Lord asked King Balaam.

'Messengers of King Balek, who wants me to join with him and fight against these people from Egypt,' King Balaam told the Lord.

'You shall not fight them for I have blessed them,' the Lord told him.

The next morning King Balaam told King Balek's messengers, 'Go back to your king and tell him, "The Lord refuses to let me fight these people because He has blessed them."'

•

King Balek Sends his Princes

King Balek's messengers went back and told their king what King Balaam had said. King Balek then sent princes more esteemed than the messengers. The princes went to King Balaam.

'Our king will do anything you say. He will give you great honours if you will help him fight these people.'

And King Balaam told them, 'If your king gave me his house full of silver and gold I could not go against what the Lord tells me. But you may spend the night here.'

But King Balaam rose in the morning and saddled his donkey and went with King Balek's princes.

The Angel Bars King Balaam's Way

God was very angry because King Balaam went and he sent an Angel who stood and barred King Balaam's way. The donkey saw the Angel of the Lord with his sword drawn and the donkey moved out of the way and into a field. King Balaam whipped the donkey to go back on the road but the Angel now stood in the fields before them and there was a wall to one side.

When the donkey saw the Angel again he became frightened and started forward and rammed into the wall and crushed King Balaam's foot. Still King Balaam whipped the donkey to continue.

Then the Angel of the Lord went farther and stood in a narrow place so that King Balaam on the donkey could not turn either to the left nor to the right. Thereupon the donkey grew more frightened and fell to the ground. King Balaam tumbled after him. The king got up and whipped the donkey to rise, but the Lord put words into the donkey's mouth.

'Why have you whipped me three times?' the donkey asked.

'Because you have made a fool of me and if I had a sword I would kill you!' King Balaam told the donkey.

'Am I not the same donkey you have always ridden? Have I not always before done as you commanded?'

Then the Angel of the Lord again stood before them. When Balaam saw the Angel he bowed his head and fell flat on his face.

●

The Angel and King Balaam

The Angel said to King Balaam, 'Why have you whipped your donkey three times? If she had not turned from me I would have slain you and saved her.'

'I have sinned,' King Balaam confessed. 'I shall return to my own country.'

'No. Go with the men,' the Angel told him. 'But you shall only say what I shall tell you.'

And King Balaam agreed and went on with the princes of King Balek.

●

Numbers 23–24

King Balaam's Prophecy

King Balaam told King Balek that the Lord now spoke for him. King Balek took him to the top of his tallest mountain and showed him his land and his people below. Then King Balaam spoke

to the Lord and when he returned to King Balek he blessed the children of Israel.

King Balek was very angry! 'I called you to fight our enemies and you bless them. Go back to your own country!'

'I told your messengers I must do as the Lord says. I will tell you what the children of Israel will do to your nation. The Lord says, "There shall come a star out of Jacob, and a sceptre shall rise out of Israel and shall destroy your land and strike down your children and conquer your country and a child of Jacob's shall become a man of great power and he shall destroy all that remains of your cities."'

Then King Balaam rose and returned to his own country and King Balek also went his own way.

•

Numbers 27

The Law of Inheritance

After many years Joseph's tribe no longer had any men to pass on their name, as only girls had been born to them. All the daughters of that tribe came before Moses.

'Our father died in the wilderness,' they told him. 'Why should the name of his family be lost because there are no longer any sons? Give us an inheritance in our father's name.'

Moses spoke to the Lord and the Lord told him, 'From this time on, if a man dies and has no sons then his inheritance shall pass to his daughters, and if he has no daughters it shall go to his brothers; and if he should have no brothers, to his father's brothers. And if his father should have no brothers, then to the next relation.'

•

Numbers 36

The Marriage of the Heiresses

Moses, speaking for the Lord, told the daughters of Joseph's tribe that they could marry whom they wished, but only to members of their father's tribe.

'So shall the inheritance,' Moses said, 'of the children of Israel not be removed from one tribe to another.'

DEUTERONOMY

The Song of Moses

When Moses was one hundred and twenty years old and the children of Israel had been wandering for forty years in search of the Promised Land, the Lord called Moses and Joshua to him and He taught Moses a song for him to bring back to the people:

> *Listen and I will speak.*
> *Listen to my words.*
> *They shall fall like small showers*
> *Upon the tender grass.*
>
> *As an eagle stirs up her nest,*
> *Flutters over her young,*
> *Spreads out her wings, takes them,*
> *Carries them on her wings—*
>
> *So the Lord alone leads Israel.*

Moses Sees Canaan

Then Moses climbed to the top of Mount Nebo and the Lord showed him all the land he was giving to each of the tribes of Israel.

'This is the land which I promised your fathers. I have let you see it with your own eyes before you die,' the Lord told Moses.

After Moses died, the people turned to Joshua, who was wise and good. But they mourned Moses for a long time. Never again in Israel was there a man like Moses who spoke to the Lord face to face and who did all the magic and wonders which Moses did in the name of the Lord.

JOSHUA

Joshua 1

God's Words to Joshua

After the death of Moses, God told Joshua, 'You shall lead the people. Every place you walk shall be yours, from the wilderness to the great river, to the greater sea and as far as the horizon. And I shall always be with you. Be strong and very courageous and observe the laws and commandments and you will be safe and successful. Your wives and your little ones and your cattle shall remain this side of Jordan but you will gather all the brave men and go onward.'

And Joshua came down from the mountain and told the people what the Lord had said to him and the people accepted Joshua as their leader.

•

Joshua 2

The Two Spies and Rahab

Joshua sent two spies to Jericho. They stopped at the house of a woman named Rahab. The King of Jericho was warned of their arrival and sent his men to her house.

'Where are the spies?' the man asked.

'There were two men who came here,' Rahab replied. 'However, they left when night came. I don't know where they were going but, since they have only left a short time ago, if you hurry you may overtake them.'

But Rahab was not telling the truth, for she had taken the two spies up to the roof of her house and hidden them there. The king's men searched for the spies all the way to the river Jordan but could not find them.

Then Rahab told the two spies, 'I know that the Lord has given you this land. All the people here fear you for that reason. They heard how the Lord dried up the waters of the Red Sea for you. For my kindness I ask you to promise no harm shall come to my father and my mother and my brothers and sisters and their families.'

'When the Lord has given us this land,' the spies said, 'we will deal kindly with you.'

•

Joshua 2

The Spies Escape

Rahab helped the spies escape. Before she left them she said, 'Go to the mountains and hide there for three days. Then go on your way.'

The men told Rahab, 'When the children of Israel come into your land you must tie a piece of scarlet ribbon to your window and bring all your family into your house. They shall all be safe unless you say a word about our business here.'

'Not one word,' Rahab said, and as soon as the two spies were out of sight she tied the piece of scarlet ribbon to the window.

•

Joshua 2

The Spies Return

The two spies went to the mountains and stayed there for three days while the king's men searched unsuccessfully for them and finally gave up the hunt and went back to the city. Then the two men came down from the mountain and crossed the river and returned to Joshua.

'What did you find?' Joshua asked.

'The people all faint with fear at the thought of us,' the men told him.

•

Joshua 3

The Parting of the Waters of the Jordan

The people moved towards Jericho. The priests went first carrying the Ark. As they came to the shores of the river Jordan, which had overflowed on to the banks because it was harvest-time, the waters stopped flowing and rose up like a wall on each side. The priests and the people passed over on dry ground and the river Jordan did not flow again until the last child of Israel had passed.

•

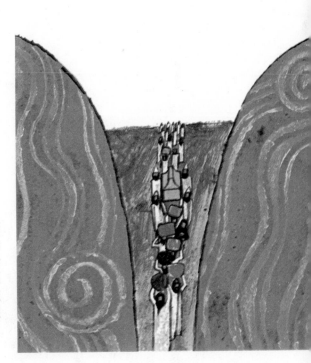

The Lord's Captain

The Walls of Jericho Fall

When Joshua and the children of Israel were near Jericho, Joshua looked up to the sky and there, above him, stood a man with a sword in his hand.

'Are you friend or enemy?' Joshua asked him.

'I am captain of the host of the Lord come to lead you,' the man said.

Joshua fell to the earth on his knees. 'What can I do for my lord?' Joshua asked.

'First take off your shoes, for the place you rest upon is holy.'

And Joshua did as the man said and the man led him forward.

•

Jericho, that great city, was kept carefully guarded. The people knew the children of Israel would come; therefore, no one went out of the city and no one came in.

The Lord had told Joshua how to capture the city and Joshua told his people. 'The priests,' he said, 'shall carry the Ark. Seven more priests shall march before them carrying seven trumpets made from rams' horns. The rest of you shall surround the city. Those who are armed will go first. You shall march silently; no sound, even on the rams' horns. And then I shall tell you to shout and to blow the horns.'

Early the next morning they circled the city and, when Joshua told them to blow their horns and shout, they did so. Then they returned to their camp. They did this for six days. On the seventh day the people in Jericho heard the sound of the trumpets and the great shouts. The walls of Jericho came tumbling down. The people of Israel walked into the city and took command.

•

Joshua 6

Rahab's Rescue

Joshua told the two who had spied for him in Jericho to go to Rahab's house and bring out Rahab and her family. The two spies did and then took Rahab and her family outside the fallen city and into the camp of the Israelites.

Joshua saved Rahab's life and her father's household and all that she had because she had hidden the messengers he had sent to spy on the city of Jericho and had spoken of it to no one.

•

The Capture of Ai

The Lord told Joshua to take all his brave men and conquer the city of Ai which was near Jericho. Joshua chose thirty thousand mighty men and sent them into the night with orders that they should wait not far from Ai and be ready when the rest of the children of Israel approached the city. Then, when the people of Ai would have seen them, they were to turn and run as if frightened of the people of Ai. The people of Ai in turn would come after them. Then when the people of Ai were away from their city, they would turn and fight them to the man and march in and take the city.

And it happened just as Joshua said it would.

•

Joshua 9

The Tattered Messengers

The people of Gibeon, not far from Ai, heard what Joshua had done to Ai and to Jericho. But they thought that if Joshua believed them to be a poor country he would not harm them. So they sent messengers dressed in tatters who carried only stale bread in their packs.

The messengers came to Joshua in his camp.

'Who are you and where do you come from?' Joshua asked.

'We have come from a distant country and we are a poor people,' the messengers replied.

Joshua looked at the tattered men and without asking the Lord's advice drew up a paper that would mean the children of Israel would not fight these poor people and swore a solemn oath to keep it. But three days later he learned the truth, for when the children of Israel reached Gibeon they saw what a rich city it was, but they would not fight because they had sworn a solemn oath.

•

The Five Kings

When the King of Jerusalem heard that Joshua had made peace with the people of Gibeon he was much afraid, because Gibeon was a rich and royal city and its men were famous for their bravery. So he called together four other kings from nearby cities to join with him to attack Gibeon.

The people in Gibeon sent a message to Joshua who was in his camp outside the city, saying, 'Come quickly and save us, for five kings who live nearby have joined together against us.'

Joshua and his army met the five smaller armies before they reached the city of Gibeon and they fought a fierce battle and Joshua won. And, as the armies fled, the Lord sent hailstones from the skies and the remaining armies of the five kings were struck down.

•

The Sun and the Moon Stand Still

Joshua then spoke to the Lord and thanked Him for His help and the Lord told him to speak to the moon and the sun.

'Sun, keep shining on Gibeon so the people can see if an enemy approaches,' he said to the sun.

'Moon, stay bright in the sky so that the enemy can be seen even there,' Joshua told the moon.

And the moon and the sun both stayed bright until the enemy no longer thought to return.

The Big War

But now Jabin, King of Hazar, heard about Joshua and he sent messengers to the north and to the south and to the east and the west, to all the kingdoms near him and they all joined together to fight Joshua and the children of Israel. There were more men than sand on the shore and many horses and chariots.

But the Lord told Joshua, 'Be not afraid of these people, for tomorrow about this time I will deliver them to you!'

It was a very big war but all the men except the children of Israel were killed that day. So Joshua took all the land and the hills and the south country and all the land of Goshen and the valley and the plain and the mountain of Israel and the valley of Lebanon under Mount Hermon. And then Joshua gave it to the children of Israel who divided it into twelve equal parts for the twelve tribes and the land rested from war.

JUDGES

The Judges

After Joshua died, Judah and Simeon and Manhasseh and many others divided the rule, but they all did many things that did not please the Lord and He grew very angry. Nevertheless, He gave the children of Israel judges to guide them.

But still they would not listen to the judges and that made the Lord even angrier.

So the children of Israel served many unjust kings for many years before a good and brave king, Ehud, came to lead them.

•

Deborah

But when Ehud died the children of Israel again went against the word of the Lord and so the Lord sold them to Jabin, King of Canaan, whose captain was Sisera and he had nine hundred chariots of iron. For twenty years the cruel Sisera ruled the children of Israel.

Now at this time there was a woman named Deborah whom the Lord had chosen as judge of the children of Israel, and she lived underneath a giant palm tree at the foot of Mount Ephraim and all the children of Israel came to her for judgment.

She sent for Barek, whom she had been watching and knew was good, and told him, 'I will cause Sisera, the captain of King Jabin's army, and his chariots and his army to come to you at the river Keshon and you will fight him and win.'

But Barek said, 'If you will come with me I shall go. But if you will not, I shall not.'

'I will go with you,' Deborah said and rose and went with Barek and his ten thousand men.

•

The Battle with Sisera

Gideon

The armies of Barek and Sisera met and the Lord defeated Sisera and his chariots and Barek killed all Sisera's men. Sisera himself got out of his chariot and fled on foot. When he reached Kadesh he stopped at the tent of Heber, who was one of King Jabin's friends. Heber's wife, Jael, came out to meet him.

'Come in,' she said. 'Do not be afraid.'

Sisera went into the tent and Jael made him lie down and covered him with a cloak.

He said, 'I am thirsty. Give me some water to drink.'

She took a bottle and gave him some milk instead and made him comfortable.

'Stand in the door of the tent,' he told her, 'and when anybody comes and asks questions say "Nobody is here." '

Then Sisera fell asleep and while he slept Jael killed him.

When Barek arrived and said 'Is anyone here?' Jael took him inside the tent and showed him the dead Sisera.

The children of Israel conquered Canaan and there was peace for the next forty years.

But once again the children of Israel went against the word of the Lord and the Lord delivered them into the cruel hands of Midian for seven years. But there was a young man named Gideon who threshed wheat in secret for his father to hide from the Midianites and on one day while he was doing so an

Angel appeared beneath an oak tree near him.

'The Lord is with you,' the Angel told Gideon, 'for you are a brave and good man.'

'If the Lord is with us why are we suffering? Where are His miracles of which our fathers told us?' Gideon asked.

'You shall go tonight and save Israel from the Midianites,' the Angel told him.

'But how? My family is poor, and I am the youngest in my father's house,' Gideon replied.

'I will be with you,' said the Angel.

Gideon's Father Speaks for him

That night Gideon took ten men and they tore down an altar to Baal, a false god, and in its place made an altar to the Lord God.

The next morning the villagers saw what Gideon had done and the men of Midian went to Gideon's father and said, 'Bring out your son. He must die.'

But Gideon's father said, 'If your god, Baal, wants to put my son to death let him speak for himself.'

And there was silence, and Gideon was spared.

The Fleece

The Spirit of the Lord came to Gideon and he blew a trumpet and all the men flocked to his side. Gideon spoke to the Lord.

'Show me a sign,' Gideon asked of the Lord. 'I shall put wool fleece on the floor and if the earth is dry and the fleece damp with dew then I will know you mean that I am to save Israel.

Gideon placed the fleece on the ground and left it there for the night. The next morning he rose early and went to where the fleece was and wrung from it a bowl of water, but the earth all around was dry!

Still he doubted. 'Do not be angry at me,' he asked of the Lord, 'but grant me one more sign. Let the fleece be dry and the earth wet.'

Again he left some fleece on the dry earth and the next morning the fleece was dry and the earth was wet!

The Three Hundred Men

Then Gideon gathered an army together from the men of Israel. They pitched their tents beside the well of Harod, so that the army of the Midianites was off to the north by a hill, but in a valley.

But God told Gideon, 'You have too many men. Tell all those you have that anyone who is afraid shall go back and not fight.'

Twenty-two thousand men went back but ten thousand stayed with Gideon. 'There are still too many men,' God told him. 'Bring them all down to the water and tell them to drink it. Separate those who lap the water with their tongues like a dog from those who kneel to drink with their hands.'

Gideon brought all the people to the water and told them to drink and of the ten thousand only three hundred lapped the water like a dog.

'Let all but the three hundred go home,' God told Gideon. 'These three hundred men will help you save Israel.'

Gideon sent all the rest of the Israelites to their tents and kept only the three hundred men.

And the army of the Midianites was below them in the valley.

The Dream

Then God told Gideon, 'Go down to the camp of the Midianites and listen to what they are saying and, afterwards, your hands will be strong for battle.'

Gideon went to the outskirts of the camp. There were so many of the enemy that they could not be counted. Gideon was silent and crept closer and he heard one man tell another a dream.

'I dreamed that a cake of barley bread tumbled into the camp of Midian. It struck a tent and the tent overturned,' the man said.

His companion told him, 'That is the sword of Gideon! God is going to let him win over us!'

Gideon went back to his men. He divided the three hundred men into three companies and he placed a trumpet in every man's hand and gave each one an empty jug with a light inside it.

'Watch me and do as I do,' he told them. 'When we come to the edge of the camp, blow your trumpets on every side of the camp and shout, "The sword of the Lord and of Gideon!" '

When they did this the enemy fled. Then the men of Israel asked Gideon to rule over them. There was peace while Gideon lived and then the children of Israel forgot the word of the law and the goodness of Gideon. And his own sons fought between them.

●

Samson

For forty years the people of Israel were slaves to the Philistines. During this time there was a man named Manoah and he had no children. The Angel of the Lord appeared to his wife and told her that she was to have a son. 'But,' the Angel said, 'you shall not cut his hair for he shall be dedicated to God from the time of his birth.'

Manoah and his wife had a son whom they called Samson, and Samson grew up tall and strong and they did not cut his hair. And when he was a grown man he went to a town called Timnath and he saw a daughter of a Philistine with whom he fell in love and wanted to marry.

At first his parents said 'No,' because they wanted him to marry one of his own people. They did not know that this marriage was part of the Lord's plans to destroy the Philistines, but when Samson insisted they agreed.

So Samson went to Tamnath with his parents. As he came near the vineyards a young lion tried to attack him and he killed it with his bare hands, but he did not tell his father and mother what he had done. They continued and he met the Philistine girl and he knew he loved her deeply.

On the way home he passed the place where the lion's body was but now the carcase of the lion was filled with a swarm of bees and honey. He took out a handful of honey and ate it and gave some to his parents, but he did not tell them that it had come from the body of the lion he had killed.

●

Samson's Riddle

The marriage of Samson and the lovely Philistine girl was planned and a wedding feast was prepared. There were thirty young Philistine men at the feast and Samson said to them, 'Here is a riddle for you and if you can solve it for me within seven days then I shall give you thirty suits of clothes, but if you fail to find the answer you must give me thirty changes of clothing.' So they said, 'Tell us your riddle.'

Samson told them, 'Out of the eater came forth meat, and out of the strong came forth sweetness.'

Three days passed and the Philistines had found no answer to the riddle. On the seventh day they said to Samson's wife, 'See if you can get your husband to tell us the answer or we will set fire to your father's house and burn you alive.'

Samson's wife wept and said to him, 'You must hate me instead of loving me for you have given my people a riddle to solve and have not told me the answer to it.'

'Neither have I told my parents,' said Samson.

His wife wept for seven days and all the time the feast was going on. At last on the seventh day Samson could bear it no longer and he told her the answer and she told her people.

Before sunset on the seventh day, the men of the city said to Samson, 'What is sweeter than honey, and what is stronger than a lion?'

His wife told him then what had happened. 'You would never have known the answer to my riddle if you had not threatened my wife,' he said. Then he

went down to Ashkelon and there he killed thirty men and took their clothes and he gave these clothes to the men who had answered his riddle. Then he went back to his father's house, terribly angry with his wife and the Philistines.

●

Samson's Anger

Then Samson wished to return to his bride, but when he came to her father's house he was told that she had been given to another man as wife. Samson's anger was great and he went into the

99

fields of the Philistines. Then he set fire to the cornfields of the Philistines so that all the corn and all the vineyards caught fire and burned up. The Philistines then moved their camps closer to Samson and told the people near there, 'We have come to capture Samson.'

Three thousand men went up to the top of the rock Etam and said to Samson, 'The Philistines will kill us all because of you. We are going to bind you and turn you over to them!'

Samson said, 'Promise me that you yourselves won't attack me.'

'No,' they said, 'but we will tie you hand and foot. And we will hand you to them.'

So they bound him with two new pieces of rope and took him to where the Philistines were. But the Spirit of the Lord descended upon Samson and the ropes became soft and fell from him. He looked around and saw a clean white bone of a donkey and with it he killed a thousand men!

Then he threw away the bone and asked the Lord for only one thing, a drink of water, for there was none to be had and he was parched with thirst. God touched a place in the rock and water gushed out of it and Samson drank his fill until his strength returned.

After that no one could stand against him and he became a judge in Israel, under the Philistines, and he judged the people for twenty years.

•

Samson's Strength

Samson fell in love with a woman named Delilah. The leaders of the Philistines came to her and said, 'Find out from him where he gets his great strength and we will give you, each of us, eleven hundred pieces of silver.'

So Delilah said to Samson, 'Tell me, I beg you, what gives you your great strength?'

'If I was bound with seven green willow stems that had never been dried I should be as weak as any other man,' Samson told her.

The leaders of the Philistines brought her seven green willow stems that had not been dried and she bound him with them. And the men were hiding in her room and she said to Samson, 'The Philistines are going to kill you, Samson!'

Samson broke the stems as if they were bits of string. So the secret of his strength was still not known.

Then Delilah said to Samson, 'You have lied to me. Tell me, I beg you, what would really securely bind you?'

And he said, 'New ropes that have never been used. Then I shall be as weak as any other man.'

Delilah took new ropes and tied him up and said to him, 'The Philistines are going to kill you, Samson!'

And again the men were hiding in the room but Samson broke the ropes again as though they were pieces of thread.

'You still tell me lies,' Delilah said. 'Tell me the truth.'

'Weave the seven locks of my hair with the web of cloth on your loom,' he said. She did it while he was sleeping and fastened it with the pin of her loom. Then she said, 'The Philistines are going to kill you, Samson!' But when he woke he easily pulled away from the pin of the loom and the web of the cloth.

•

Judges 16

The Secret

'How can you claim to love me when you tell me lies three times?' Delilah said to him. And she scolded him every day. And he loved Delilah very much and it upset him to see her unhappy. So finally he told her his secret.

'I have never cut my hair,' he said to her, 'for I have been dedicated to God since I was born. If my head was shaved my strength would go from me and I would become weak and like any other man.'

Delilah knew then that this was the real secret and she called the lords of the Philistines and they came up bringing her the money they had promised her.

Delilah made Samson go to sleep and his head was on her knees. Then she called for a barber and he shaved of seven locks of Samson's hair. Then she said, 'The Philistines are going to kill you, Samson!'

He awoke but he did not know the power of the Lord was gone from him. The Philistines quickly took him and they put out his eyes and bound him with brass chains and put him in prison.

•

Samson's Revenge

But gradually his hair began to grow again and the Philistines did not notice. They had a great festival to celebrate the capture of Samson and they said, 'Bring Samson forth so that he can entertain us.'

They brought Samson out of the prison and made fun of him. When they stood him up between two pillars, the blind Samson said to the boy who led him by the hand, 'Let me feel the pillars which support the house so that I may lean upon them.'

Now the house was filled with all the great leaders of the Philistines. There were about three thousand men and women on the roof watching while they were making fun of Samson.

Then Samson called out to the Lord, 'O Lord God, remember me and give me back my strength, just this once!'

Then Samson took hold of the two middle pillars upon which the house stood and which held it up. He held one with his right hand and the other with his left hand.

Samson said, 'Let me die with the Philistines,' and he bowed himself and pushed with all his might against the pillars and the building fell upon all the people who were inside. And all of the people were killed – and Samson with them.

RUTH

Ruth, the Faithful

During the time that the Judges ruled there was a great famine in the land and a woman named Naomi and her husband and their two sons left their own country and travelled to the country of Moab. There they lived very well and the two sons married Moab women. One girl was named Orpah and the other Ruth.

Orpah and Ruth lived happily with their husbands for ten years, and then their husbands died, as did Naomi's husband, and so Naomi decided that she would return to her own people.

'Go,' she told her daughters-in-law. 'Return to your own homes and pray to your gods, and may you each find the happiness that you gave my sons.'

But Ruth refused to leave Naomi, and so she and Naomi returned together to Bethlehem for the time of the spring harvest.

Ruth Meets Boaz

Naomi had a wealthy kinsman, the brother of her dead husband, and his name was Boaz. Ruth went to glean the last of the grain in the fields that belonged to Boaz. One day Boaz came into the field and he saw Ruth. 'Who is that?' he asked his servants.

'That is Ruth, the widow, and the daughter-in-law of Naomi,' they said.

Boaz was much taken by Ruth and he said to her, 'Let your eyes remain on your work and not on the young men in the fields and I will see that no one dares harm you.'

And Boaz invited her to eat with him and she did and then Ruth left and went back to the city with her gleaning and told Naomi about her meeting with Boaz. Naomi was pleased and bid Ruth to do as Boaz said.

So Ruth gathered grain in the fields of Boaz, doing as he had told her, and each night she returned to the city where she lived with Naomi.

●

Naomi Tells Ruth what to do

At the end of the wheat harvest Naomi said to Ruth, 'My daughter, you must now find rest and a new life. Boaz is good and wealthy and he is a kinsman. Tonight he shall be in the threshing room where they separate the wheat from the stalks. He will work and eat and sleep there and when he is asleep you shall lie down at his feet and when he wakes he will tell you what you shall do.'

So Ruth went into the threshing room and hid. Boaz ate and drank until his heart was merry, then he went to sleep at the end of the heap of grain. Then Ruth came softly and laid down at his feet.

At midnight Boaz woke and saw Ruth. 'Who are you?' he asked her in the darkness.

'I am Ruth,' she said quickly.

'You are blessed,' he told her, 'for you have not looked at the young men, rich or poor, and you have remained with your mother-in-law, Naomi, and followed your dead husband's faith. All the people of Bethlehem know you are a good woman. Stay tonight and in the morning I will make arrangements for your future.'

Ruth lay at his feet until the morning and then she rose and Boaz said, 'Bring your veil to me and hold it out.'

When she did so, he placed six measures of barley into the veil. Ruth brought this back to Naomi.

'Wait patiently,' Naomi told her. 'This man will not rest until you are his wife.'

●

Boaz Marries Ruth

That day Boaz met with the rest of Naomi's kinsmen and spoke to the one closest to her.

'Naomi is selling a piece of land which belonged to our brother, her husband,' he told him. 'I think you should buy it before it goes out of the family. But if you do not wish to, tell me now, so that I can have the next right to buy it, for if you buy the land you must also marry Ruth, the widow of Naomi's son.'

'I cannot,' the man said. 'You can have my rights.'

Boaz turned to the others. 'You are witnesses that I have bought from Naomi all that belonged to our brother and to his sons and I have claimed Ruth to be my wife,' he said.

'We are witnesses,' they replied, 'and may the Lord bless your house and make it famous in Bethlehem.'

And Boaz and Ruth were married and Ruth had a little boy, and the women in the town all came to Naomi and said, 'Blessed be the name of the Lord, who has not left you without an heir and may he be a famous man when he is grown. He shall surely make you feel young again and care for you in your old age, for he is Ruth's son and she loves you better than seven sons.'

And Naomi helped Ruth care for the little boy and the child was called Obed. He became the father of Jesse, who was the father of David.

•

FIRST BOOK OF SAMUEL

I Samuel 1

The Birth of Samuel

There was a woman named Hannah whose husband, Elkanah, loved her dearly. But Hannah was always sad because she did not have a child. One day she went to the temple of the priest, Eli. She prayed there for a child and she promised that if she had a child she would give him to the Lord to serve Him. Eli, the priest, saw her but he could not hear what she was saying for she was praying silently.

'You shall have what you have prayed for,' Eli told her, and Hannah left the temple, no longer sad.

Hannah did have a son and she called him Samuel. And when Samuel no longer needed his mother to feed him, Hannah took him to the temple of Eli.

The Sin of Eli's Sons

Now the sons of Eli, the priest, were not good men and did not believe in the Lord's word. But Samuel grew to be a young boy who followed the Lord. And every year Hannah made him a little coat and brought it to him.

When Eli grew very old he heard about the evil dealings of his own sons and it troubled him greatly.

'I have heard bad reports,' he told them. 'You must remember if one man sins against the other a judge can judge him, but when he sins against the Lord he can answer only to the Lord.'

But Eli's sons would not listen.

•

God Calls Samuel

As Eli grew old he grew blind and young Samuel became his eyes. One night when Eli had gone to sleep, Samuel lay down to rest and he heard the voice of the Lord, but he thought it was Eli calling him and he ran to him.

'I did not call you,' Eli said. 'Lie down again.'

So Samuel again lay down to rest but again he heard a voice call him. Samuel arose and ran to Eli.

'Here I am. You called me,' he said.

'I did not, my son,' Eli replied. 'Lie down again.'

When the Lord called Samuel for the third time, Samuel arose and went to Eli but Eli understood that the Lord was calling the boy. Therefore he said, 'Go lie down and, when you hear a voice call you again, you will say, "Speak, Lord, and I will listen".'

So Samuel went back to lie in his small bed and the Lord came and stood beside him and called again. This time Samuel stood up.

'Speak, my Lord, and I will listen,' he said.

The Lord said to Samuel, 'Eli's sons have gone against my word and Eli did not stop them. Therefore, I will judge this house.'

Then the Lord went away and Samuel lay until morning without sleeping because he was afraid to tell Eli what the Lord had said. But in the morning Eli called him and Samuel arose and went to him.

'What did the Lord say to you?' Eli asked.

And Samuel told him and Eli said, 'The Lord God's word is law.'

●

I Samuel 3–4

The Ark is Stolen

All Israel knew that the Lord had chosen to speak to Samuel, so Samuel became the man who spoke the Lord's words to the people.

During this time the children of Israel went to war against the Philistines but in their first battle four thousand of their men were killed. They sent messengers

to Eli's temple to bring the Ark from the temple to the battlefield, which was against the law of the Lord. Eli's two sons were guarding the Ark when the messengers came and they let the Ark go out of the temple.

When the Ark arrived in the camp the men shouted with joy. The Philistines knew the Hewbrews had brought the Ark to the camp and they were afraid. Still, they attacked the children of Israel. It was a mighty battle and thirty thousand children of Israel were killed. Then the Philistines stole the Ark and killed Eli's two sons.

When Eli heard from a tattered soldier about the great slaughter and the death of his sons and the stealing of the Ark by the Philistines, the shock was so great and he was so old that he died of a broken heart.

●

110

The Plague of the Philistines

The Ark is Returned

The Philistines brought the Ark of God into the temple of Dagon, a false god that was a statue, and set it beside Dagon. When the Philistines arose early the next morning they went straight to the temple of Dagon and found he had fallen to the ground, his face buried in the earth before the Ark.

They picked him up and set him back in his place.

The next morning when they returned, Dagon had again fallen to the ground – but this time not only was his face buried in the earth but his hands had been separated from the rest of him.

The priests of Dagon were frightened because they knew the Hand of the Israelites' God was now upon them. So they decided to remove the Ark of the God of Israel and send it to another city called Ekron. But the Ekronites cried, 'Why have you brought us the Ark of the God of Israel? We will all be killed!'

Then they called together all the high lords of the Philistines and said, 'Send away the Ark of the God of Israel and let it go again to His own temple so that it won't kill us all!'

But the Ark remained and the city was struck by a great plague. And the cry of the city went up to heaven.

The Ark remained with the Philistines for seven months, and the plague continued. Then they went to their priests. 'What shall we do?' they asked.

And the priests replied, 'Send away the Ark and with it an offering.'

'What shall the offering be?' the people asked.

'Five golden mice,' the priests told them. 'Then make a new cart and tie two milk cows to it with no yoke and take the Ark of the Lord and lay it upon the cart and put the golden mice in a box by its side and send it away with the cows to lead it.'

The Philistines did this and the cows took a straight path, turning neither left nor right, to the border of Beth-shemesh. The farmers of Beth-shemesh were reaping their wheat and they looked up and saw the Ark and they rejoiced at seeing it! But they opened the box and took out the five golden mice and the men of Beth-shemesh made offerings to them. The Lord made the men of Beth-shemesh suffer mightily because they had looked into the Ark and prayed to false gods.

•

I Samuel 7

The End of the Philistines

Samuel said, 'Return to the Lord. Serve Him only and He will deliver you from the Philistines.'

The people put away all false gods and served the Lord alone and Samuel told them, 'I will pray for you to the Lord.'

All the people gathered together at Mizpeh and fasted the entire day and said, 'We have sinned against the Lord!'

The Philistines heard that the children of Israel were gathered together at Mizpeh and they attacked them, but as the Philistines drew near the Lord thundered, and most of their men were killed and the men of Israel turned away the rest.

The cities they had taken from Israel were returned, and Samuel remained a judge to his people and he travelled from one city to another to judge for them, but he always returned to Ramah, where he lived.

•

I Samuel 8

The People Want a King

Samuel was now growing old and his sons were not as good as he, and took bribes as judges so that justice was not always done. The older people of Israel were worried that Samuel would die and so they came to him saying, 'Your sons are not as good judges as you. Give us a king to judge us.'

Samuel spoke to the Lord and then told the people, 'If you have a king he will take your sons to drive his chariots. He will make himself captain over all of them and make them reap his harvests and fight his wars. He will take your daughters as servants and they will do his work.'

Nevertheless, the people still wanted a king over them. 'We will have a king over us,' they told Samuel. 'Then we will be like other nations and our king may judge us and fight our battles.'

Samuel told the Lord what the people said.

'Make them a king,' the Lord said.

So Samuel told the people, 'All of you go back to your own cities.'

•

Saul and the Donkeys

There was a man named Kish and he had a son named Saul who was brighter and taller than most of the other children of Israel. One day some donkeys belonging to Kish were lost and Kish sent Saul and a servant to look for them. They travelled a long way and did not find the donkeys, so Saul told the servant, 'We shall turn back so that my father will not worry that we are lost as well.'

But the servant suggested they go into the nearby city and speak to the man of God who lived there and perhaps he could tell them which direction they should take.

'A good idea,' Saul said. 'Come, let us go.'

So they went toward the city to find the man of God and as they were going up the hill to the city they saw some young girls drawing water from a well.

'Is the man of God here?' Saul asked.

'He is,' they replied, 'but be quick, for he will soon leave for the mountain to pray.'

They went into the city and met Samuel on his way up the mountain.

Now, the Lord had told Samuel a day before, 'Tomorrow at this time I will send a man out of the land of Benjamin and you shall make him captain over my people and he will save them from the Philistines.'

When Samuel saw Saul the Lord said to Samuel, 'Behold! That is the man. He shall reign over my people.'

Saul said to Samuel, 'Can you tell me where I can find Samuel?'

'I am Samuel. Go up before me to the mountaintop and eat with me today and tomorrow. I will tell you all that is in your heart, and as for the donkeys that were lost three days ago, they have been found.'

Saul ate with Samuel and when they came back into the city he stayed with Samuel in Samuel's house. They arose early the next morning and as they were going down to the end of the city Samuel said to Saul, 'Bid your servant walk before us but you stand still so that I can show you the word of God.'

I Samuel 10

Samuel's Words to Saul

'The Lord has appointed you captain over all his people. When you leave me today you will find two men by Rachel's tomb on the border of the land of Israel and they will say to you, "The donkeys you went to look for have been found but your father is now worried about you". You shall continue on and come to the plain of Tabor and there you will meet three men, one carrying three kids, the second three loaves of bread and the third a bottle of wine. They will greet you and give you two loaves of bread which you shall take. After that you will come to the hill of God where you will also find the garrison of the Philistines. And as you draw near you will meet a group of priests coming down the mountain and they will have a lute, a tambourine, a pipe and a harp and they shall foretell your future.'

'The spirit of the Lord will come to you and you shall become another man. And let it be when these signs come to you that you serve God, for God is with you. And then you shall go down to Gilgal and I will be there to meet you seven days later and show you what you are to do next.'

And all these signs came to pass that very day, exactly as Samuel told Saul they would.

●

I Samuel 10–13

Saul is Chosen King

Then Samuel brought together all the tribes of Israel. But at first Saul could not be found. But when he did appear, he stood among the people and he was a head taller than any of them.

Samuel said to all the people, 'This is whom the Lord has chosen to be your king.'

'God save the king!' the people shouted.

Then Samuel sent the people to their homes and Saul went home as well and with him went a band of men whose hearts God had touched. But there were some who asked, 'How shall this man save us?'

But Saul held the peace and became a great king and a very brave soldier and led the children of Israel into many battles against the Philistines. But he began to disobey the word of the Lord and Samuel told him, 'The Lord would have kept your kingdom over Israel for ever but now your kingdom will not continue.'

•

Samuel Finds David

But Saul still went against the word of the Lord and when he won a battle he took the sheep and oxen and lambs of the losers, whereas God had told him not to do so. Samuel came to Saul and told him he had done wrong, and they parted with bitter words.

Then the Lord spoke to Samuel, 'I have taken the kingdom away from Saul and provided a new king, one of the sons of Jesse (the grandson of Ruth and Boaz). Go to Jesse and tell him.'

'How can I go?' Samuel asked. 'If Saul hears it he will kill me.'

'I shall be with you,' the Lord said.

So Samuel went to Jesse and he had all seven of his sons passed before Samuel but none of them was the one the Lord had chosen to be king. 'Are these *all* your children?' he asked Jesse.

'There is still my youngest son,' Jesse told him. 'He tends the sheep.'

'Bring him here,' Samuel told Jesse.

Jesse sent for the boy. He was a handsome lad and the Lord told Samuel, 'Arise, for this is he.'

The boy's name was David and Samuel rose up and went home and the spirit of the Lord touched David. But the spirit of the Lord left Saul.

•

David Plays the Harp

Saul became ill and his servants came to him and said, 'If a man could play the harp beautifully for you, you would get better.'

'Find such a man and bring him to me,' Saul said.

One of the servants told him, 'I remember such a musician. He is the youngest son of Jesse.'

Saul then sent messengers to Jesse and said, 'Send me David, your son.'

And David came to Saul and stood before him and he played and Saul was cured almost from the first note; and he loved David like a son and made him his armour bearer.

•

I Samuel 17

David and Goliath

Now the Philistines gathered their armies and went to battle against Israel, and Saul gathered his army and they pitched their tents. The Philistines stood on the mountain on the other side and there was a valley between them.

Then Goliath, who was over ten feet tall, came out of the camp of the Philistines. He had a helmet of brass upon his head and was armed in a coat of heavy brass and had more brass around his legs and between his shoulders. The staff of his spear was huge and the head of it weighed six hundred pounds, and he carried a shield as well.

He stood looking over the valley and cried to the army of Israel, 'Choose a man among you and let him come to fight me. And if he is able to fight me and kill me, then all the Philistines will be your servants. But if I kill him, then you shall be our servants and serve us.'

When the men of Israel saw Goliath they were afraid, but David was not.

Saul sent for David and David told Saul, 'I will fight Goliath.'

'You cannot, for Goliath has been a man of war since his youth and you are still a boy,' Saul told him.

But David replied, 'While I kept my father's sheep, a lion came and took a lamb from the flock and I went after him and hit him and took the lamb from his mouth. Then I caught him by his beard and hit him again and killed him. If I can kill a lion I can kill Goliath. The Lord saved me from the paw of the lion. He will save me from the hand of this Philistine.'

'Go then,' Saul told him, 'and God be with you.'

David Fights Goliath

Saul armed David with his armour and put a helmet of brass upon his head and also armed him with a coat of brass. And David told Saul, 'I cannot wear these, for I have never worn armour before,' and removed them. Then he took his staff in his hand and chose five smooth stones from the brook and put them in a bag and took his sling and went towards Goliath.

When Goliath saw David he laughed, for David was but an unarmed boy, and he advanced to kill David.

'You come at me with a sword and a spear,' David said, 'but I come to you in the name of the Lord and the armies of the Lord which you have defied.'

Goliath started towards David and David put his hand in his bag and took out a stone and put it in his sling and slung it and struck Goliath on his forehead. Goliath fell dead on the earth.

When the Philistines saw that Goliath was dead, they fled.

Jonathan and David

David and Jonathan became as close as two brothers and Jonathan gave David his own robe and his sword and his bow. David did whatever Saul asked of him and behaved wisely, and Saul then made him an officer over the men at war, by whom David was accepted and loved. So much so, that, when he came back into the city, the women met him, singing his praises and dancing and playing tambourines and other musical instruments. They praised David *more* than they praised Saul and Saul became very jealous of David, because he feared the people would make David king even over himself.

Saul's Jealousy

Saul was afraid of David because the Lord was with him and no longer with Saul, so he thought of a plan. 'I will give you my eldest daughter, Merab,' he said to David, 'but you must be very brave and fight the Lord's battles.' Saul thought David would then be killed in battle.

David was very humble. 'Who am I or my father's family in Israel,' he asked, 'that I should be son-in-law to the king?'

But Merab loved another, and Saul's younger daughter, Michal, loved David truly and David loved her and they told this to Saul. This pleased Saul very much, for he thought if David loved Michal so much he would try to be even braver against the Philistines and would *surely* be killed. So he said to David, 'You shall be my son-in-law!' And then he spoke secretly to his servants and told them to tell David, 'The king is pleased with you and all the people love you. Marry Michal and become the king's son-in-law.'

When the servants told David this he

replied, 'It is not right that a poor man like me of lowly birth should be the king's son-in-law.

The servants told Saul what David had said and Saul told them to tell David this: 'The king does not wish any money for his daughter's hand, but instead one hundred Philistines to be killed in battle.' For Saul thought David would thus be killed.

But David went out and killed *two* hundred Philistines in battle and Saul promised him Michal for his wife. Saul knew the Lord was with David and that his daughter, Michal, loved David very much and this made him more afraid, and he began to think of David as the real enemy and not the Philistines.

•

Michal Saves David's Life

Then Saul spoke to Jonathan and asked him to kill David, but Jonathan loved David and so he told him, 'My father wants to kill you. Therefore be careful until morning and hide so that neither he nor his servants will find you. I will try to talk to my father meanwhile.'

And Jonathan told Saul, 'Do not commit this sin against David. He has not sinned against you. He put his life in danger and killed the Philistines. You cannot kill David without cause.'

Saul told Jonathan, 'You are right By God's name, David shall live.'

Then Jonathan told David what Saul had said and David came to Saul. When Saul had his spear in his hand and David played his music, Saul raised the spear and threw it at David. But David moved

aside just in time and the spear struck the wall behind him, and David escaped over the wall and to his house.

But Michal knew her father would have David killed that night, so she helped him escape. That night, after he was gone, she placed a statue in David's bed and covered it over and when Saul sent messengers to David, Michal was there to greet them and said, 'David is sick.'

But Saul had the bed carried to his throne room and when he saw what Michal had done he asked her, 'Why have you deceived me and let my enemy escape?'

'Because he would have killed me otherwise,' Michal lied.

David, meantime, had reached Samuel in Ramah and told him what Saul had tried to do.

●

I Samuel 20

David and Jonathan Part

David made his way back again to see Jonathan. 'What have I done,' he asked him, 'that your father should want to kill me?'

'He is envious of your fame,' Jonathan told him. 'But nothing will happen to you. My father loves me as I love you and he will tell me if he has a plan to kill you.'

'Yes, that is so, but as the Lord lives, there is just one small step between me and death!'

'If my father plans an evil deed I shall tell you. Still, tomorrow is the new moon. You shall stay three days by the stone Ezel and I will come and shoot three arrows in its side for a mark. Then, I will say to my boy-servant, "The arrows are on the side of the stone. Go find them." Then you will know you are safe. But if I say, "The arrows are *beyond* the stone," go away, David, because you will be in danger.'

So David hid in a field and the new moon came out. He hid for three days in this place and Jonathan spoke to his father and pleaded for David's life.

Saul grew very angry. 'Don't you know that as long as David lives you shall never be king after me?'

'I do not wish to be king if it means David's murder,' Jonathan told his father.

Saul grew angrier at this and he hurled his sword at Jonathan, just missing him. And Jonathan rose from the table in fierce anger and left his father's house. He waited until the third morning and then took his boy-servant and his bow and went to the field near the stone Ezel and shot three arrows into the side. But as the lad went to fetch them, he shot another arrow and then called out loudly, *'The arrow is beyond you!'* The lad gathered the arrows and came back and Jonathan sent him back to the city.

But as soon as the lad was gone, David came out of his hiding-place and Jonathan and David embraced. Then David went his way and Jonathan returned to the city.

●

I Samuel 23–25

David Spares Saul's Life

And David went to stay with the priests of Nob and Saul followed him and killed the priests. Then many of the people joined

with David. When the Philistines attacked a city, David and his band of men would fight them. One city he saved was the city of Keilah. And when Saul heard David was in that city he gathered his men to attack his own city to kill David.

But David heard that Saul was coming to Keilah and so he took his band of six hundred men from the city and travelled into the wilderness in the mountains of Ziph where Saul could not find him.

But Saul learned that David had moved from the mountains of Ziph to the caves of Engedi, and he took three thousand men with him to find him.

Saul came to the caves and, weary from travel, went inside one and lay down to rest. And David found him there. David lifted his sword to strike Saul but he could not kill this man who was his king and his sword only tore away part of Saul's robe.

Saul woke and saw David who stooped to the ground, saying, 'My lord, the king!' Then he rose. 'How could you think I would harm you?' he asked. 'Just now I raised my sword but I could not kill you and only tore your robe with my blade. For you were chosen king by the Lord and I could never raise my hand against you.'

When Saul heard these words and looked at David, he wept. 'You are more righteous than I, for you have rewarded me with good and I have rewarded you with evil. Now, behold, I know you will surely be king and that the kingdom of Israel shall be yours. But swear before me, by the Lord, that my name will not be destroyed!'

David swore this to Saul and then Saul went home.

Second Book Of Samuel

II Samuel 1

David Hears of Saul's Death

Saul had continued to fight the Philistines. One day a young man came out of Saul's camp with his clothes torn and came to David and fell before him to the ground.

'Where have you come from?' David asked.

'I have escaped from Saul's camp,' the young man replied.

'What happened there?' David asked.

'There was a terrible battle and those who did not die, fled. And Saul and Jonathan, his son, are also dead.'

'How do you know they are dead?'

The young man then told David, 'As I happened by chance to come to Mount Gilboa I saw Saul leaning on his spear, more dead that alive. When he saw me he called to me and I went to his side. "Who are you?" he asked. "I am an Amalekite" I told him. "Kill me, for I am in great pain!" he begged. And I killed him, for I knew he could not live long. Then I took the crown that was on his head and the bracelet that was on his arm and have brought them to you.'

'And Jonathan?'

'Jonathan fell in battle.'

David mourned Saul, for he had been made king of Israel by the Lord; and he mourned Jonathan, for he had been more than his brother.

•

II Samuel 3

David, King of Judah

David was made King of Judah and he and his men lived in the cities of Hebron. But Ishbosheth, who was one of Saul's sons, was made king over all Israel, and Abner was his champion who fought for him. There was a long war between Ishbosheth and David, but David grew stronger and stronger and Ishbosheth became weaker and weaker. But in Ishbosheth's house Abner became as strong as Ishbosheth and then Ishbosheth and Abner had a terrible fight and Abner told him, 'I will turn this kingdom over to David so he shall rule over Israel and Judah!' And Ishbostheth was now too frightened of Abner to reply.

Then Abner sent messengers to David, saying, 'Make a pact with me and I shall bring all Israel under your rule.'

And David told him, 'I shall do so but I ask one thing of you before I will even see you. Bring Michal, Saul's daughter, with you when you come.'

Michal was taken from the husband to whom she was wed after David had fled.

And he went with her for part of the journey and wept when he left her. Then Abner went on to David.

•

Abner and Joab at the Gate

Abner went to all the tribes of Israel and gathered them together to make a pact with David. But there was a man named Joab whose father Abner had killed in battle. And while Abner was returning to David after seeing all the tribes, Joab took Abner aside by a gate to speak quietly to him and there struck Abner and killed him to avenge his brother's death.

David mourned Abner's death and he told his men, 'A prince, a great man, has fallen this day in Israel and, because of it, this day I am weaker.'

•

II Samuel 5

David Becomes King Over All Israel

All the tribes of Israel then came to David and made him king over all Israel. He was then only thirty years old and he reigned for forty years. He took Zion, which became the city of David, and the people built him a house. And he grew great and the Lord was with him.

When the Philistines heard that David was now king they came and spread out in the valleys around Zion.

David asked the Lord, 'Shall I fight the Philistines?'

'Yes,' said the Lord. 'I shall deliver them into your hands.'

David fought the Philistines and won and he burned all the false idols they left behind when they fled.

•

A House for God

The Lord spoke to the prophet Nathan, telling him 'I have not lived in any house since I brought the children of Israel out of Egypt but have walked in a tent with all the children of Israel. Now you shall build Me a house of cedar.'

Nathan spoke to David, repeating the Lord's words. And David had a house of cedar built for the Lord.

David reigned over all Israel and gave the people his wisdom and judged their sins.

•

II Samuel 9

Jonathan's Son

(*Jonathan's little son was five years old when Jonathan was killed. The child's nurse ran away with him to save him from the Philistines. But as she ran she fell, and the boy, whose name was Mephiboseth, was injured and the boy was thereafter lame.*)

David asked of the people, 'Is there yet any left of the house of Saul that I may show him kindness for Jonathan's sake?'

There was a servant named Ziba. And Ziba told David, 'Jonathan had a son who is lame.'

'Where is he?' David asked.

Ziba told him and David sent for Mephiboseth. And when Jonathan's son came before David, he bowed to the floor.

'Do not be afraid,' David told him. 'I will be kind to you for I loved your father and will give you back all the land that was his and his father's, and you shall stay with me.'

So Mephiboseth stayed with David and ate always at his table.

•

II Samuel 11

David and Bathsheba

One evening David awoke and walked upon the roof of the palace and from the roof he saw a woman washing herself, and she was very beautiful.

David asked about the woman and found that she was Bathsheba, the wife of Uriah. He sent messengers to her and she came to see him. David knew that he loved Bathsheba, so he sent for Joab to put Uriah into the very heat of the next battle. Joab did so and Uriah was killed in battle.

When Bathsheba heard of her husband's death she mourned him. And when the mourning was past, David sent and fetched her to his house and she became his wife and had a son. But the Lord was very displeased with what David had done.

•

II Samuel 13

Absalom Kills his Brother

David had many children by his wives and, among them, Absalom was his favourite son. Absalom had a beautiful sister, who was born of the same mother, and her name was Tamar. Amnon, another of David's sons, was jealous of Absalom and, after a time, came to hate his sister Tamar more than he loved her or his father and he was evil to her and then threw her out of his house. Tamar returned crying to Absalom's house. And Absalom and Amnon had a terrible fight and Amnon was killed.

David's other sons pleaded for Absalom. David knew that Amnon had done wrong to his sister, Tamar. He longed to comfort Absalom because he loved the young man very much. But Absalom was banished from Jerusalem and was gone three years, and David mourned every day that the young man was away.

Joab sent a widow woman to David and

she told him a story about her own two sons that was very similar to that which had happened between Absalom and Amnon and then asked David to judge. But David guessed that Joab had sent the woman and put the words in the woman's mouth so that David would see it was unjust for Absalom to remain banished from Jerusalem.

David called Joab and told him, 'Bring Absalom back to Jerusalem and tell him he may live in his own house, but he is never to see or speak to me.'

So Absalom was brought home by Joab, but he did not see or speak to David.

Joab and Absalom

But in all Israel there was not a young man more handsome than Absalom. He was perfect, from the crown of his head to the soles of his feet. Still, Absalom lived in Jerusalem for two years and David did not set eyes upon him.

Absalom was longing to see his father, so he sent messengers to Joab but Joab refused to come. Again he sent messengers and still Joab refused to come to Absalom so Absalom had his servants set fire to Joab's barley field and Joab came to Absalom saying, 'Why have your servants set my field on fire?'

'So that you would come to me and then I could ask you to beg my father to see me.'

Joab went to David and spoke a second time for Absalom. Then Joab called Absalom and Absalom came to his father and bowed himself to the ground before him. David then told his son to rise and looked into his handsome face and kissed him.

•

David Mourns his Son

Soon all Israel came to David for judgment, but saw Absalom instead. They grew to love him dearly, for his judgments were always fair.

Then one day Absalom came to David and told him, 'I made a vow when I was banished from Jerusalem that I would serve the Lord. Now that I have been reconciled with you, I want to keep that vow.'

'Go in peace,' David told him.

But Absalom went out in battle for the Lord and did many things that were not right. He turned some of the people against his father and then joined the enemy and soon there was a great war.

David wanted to go to battle but the people told him, 'Do not go. You are worth ten thousand of us; it is better if you stay in the city.'

'What the people feel is best I shall do,' David replied. So he stood by the gate of the city and the people came out by the hundreds and by the thousands and David commanded Joab, 'Deal gently for my sake with the young man, Absalom!' And all the people heard this order about Absalom.

Then the people fought a terrible battle with the enemy and many of those who fought were killed but the Israelites won and Absalom fled from them on the back of a mule. The mule went under the thick boughs of a great oak and Absalom's head was caught and he was lifted from the back of the mule and hung there.

A soldier saw this and went to Joab and told him. Joab said to the man, 'Why did you not kill him, for he is our enemy?'

'The king commanded that none should touch the young man, Absalom,' the soldier said. 'I heard him.'

But Joab went to where Absalom was caught and he shot an arrow and killed him. The he blew his trumpet and the people who were left came and cut Absalom down and buried him there.

Then a messenger was sent to David to tell him his son was dead and the king went to a small chamber and wept, crying: 'O my son, Absalom, my son, my son! Absalom! Would God I had died for you! O Absalom, my son, my son!'

•

II Samuel 19

King David and his People

The victory that day was turned into mourning and the people all heard the king's cries and the people were ashamed.

Joab came to the king and said, 'It seems to the people that you love your enemies and hate your friends, for if Absalom had lived and your people had all died, it would have pleased you more. You must stop this mourning and comfort your people instead, or worse evil than the loss of the king's son will happen this day.'

So the king arose and went to the gate of the city and put away his mourning to comfort his people.

And the people now loved King David even more.

FIRST BOOK OF KINGS

I Kings 1

David's Last Words

David grew very old and remained in his bed. Absalom's younger brother, Adonijah – who was a good man – made himself king without speaking to his father, and many of the people followed him.

But Nathan the prophet and Solomon, Bathsheba's son, did not. So Nathan spoke to Bathsheba, 'I will give you counsel,' he said, 'so that you may save your own life and the life of your son, Solomon. Go to the king's bedchamber and say to him, "Did you not swear to me that our son Solomon would one day sit on the throne? Why then does Adonijah reign?" Then I will come into his room while you are still there and tell him this is so.'

And so Bathsheba went to the king's bedchamber and bowed to him. 'What am I to do for you?' the king asked.

'My lord,' Bathsheba said to him, 'you swore that our son, Solomon, would reign after you and sit upon your throne but, though you do not know it, another son, Adonijah, is reigning already. If you do not tell the people of Israel who shall sit on your throne before you die, then Solomon and I will be cast out.'

Then Nathan entered the bedchamber, 'My lord,' he said, 'have you said Adonijah shall reign after you and sit upon your throne? For he has called the people together but not me or Solomon, and the people have said, "God save King Adonijah".'

The king was quite angry that Adonijah would do this without telling him first. 'Bathsheba,' he called.

'Yes, my lord?' Bathsheba said, as she came close to his bedside.

'I will declare to the people today that Solomon shall sit upon my throne in my place,' he said to her.

Bathsheba bowed deeply. 'I wish the lord King David would live for ever,' she told him.

David then told Nathan, 'Take my servants and give Solomon my mule and bring him down to Gihon, and there anoint him king over Israel and blow your trumpet and say "God save King Solomon." Then bring him here so that he can sit upon my throne and be king in my place.'

Solomon, the King

Nathan did as David charged him and brought Solomon to Gihon and there anointed him and blew a trumpet and called out, 'God save King Solomon!'

Then all the people came to Solomon and played on their pipes and rejoiced.

But Adonijah was entertaining at this time and all his guests heard the sound of the people and Joab asked, 'What is this noise I hear?'

And he was told, 'King David has made Solomon king, and Solomon was brought to his bedside and Solomon bowed to David and our lord King David said, "God, make the name of Solomon greater than my own and make his throne greater than my throne," and then King David bowed from his bed to Solomon.'

All Adonijah's guests were afraid then and rose and every man went his way. Adonijah was also frightened, for he thought Solomon would kill him.

But Solomon said, 'If Adonijah remains a worthy man not a hair on his head shall be touched, but if he does evil then he shall die.'

Adonijah was then brought before Solomon and Solomon told him to go to his house without fear unless he went against the law of God.

Solomon Asks for Wisdom

Before David died he told Solomon: 'Be strong and walk in the Lord God's ways and obey His laws.' Then he died and was buried in the city of David.

Then the Lord appeared at night to Solomon in a dream. 'Ask what I shall give you,' the Lord said.

'O Lord, my God, You have made me king but I am still a boy and know not what to do. Give me, therefore, an understanding heart to judge my people so that I can know good from bad,' Solomon said.

The Lord was pleased with Solomon. 'Because you have asked for wisdom and not for riches I will be with you and you shall have a wise and understanding heart, and though you have not asked you shall also have riches and honour and there will be no king like you while you live.'

●

Solomon's Judgment

Two women came before King Solomon and one woman told him, 'I live in a house with this woman you see beside me, and I had a child there and this

131

woman had a child there as well and we were alone with no strangers. Then this woman's child died in the night and she awoke at midnight and took my son and laid her own dead son in his place, and when I awoke I saw the dead child and knew it was not mine.'

And the other woman said, 'No! The living son is my son! The dead child is her son!'

'Bring me a sword!' the king commanded.

And they brought a sword to the king.

'Divide the living child in two and give half to one woman and half to the other,' he said.

But the first woman cried out, 'O my lord! Don't harm the child! Give the living child to this woman!'

And the second woman said, 'Let it be dead so that neither of us shall have a child!'

Solomon gave the child to the first woman. 'Give her the living child,' he said. 'She is the mother.'

And the child and its real mother were reunited and all the people of Israel heard of the judgment and knew this wisdom of God was with Solomon. And all the people from the kingdoms all over the earth came to hear the wisdom of Solomon.

●

I Kings 6–8

A Temple for God

When Solomon had reigned for four years he began to build a temple for the Lord. It was made of stone on the outside and cedar wood on the inside and all the work was done away from the building site so that there would be no noise. Then Solomon had an altar built completely covered in pure gold. All the doors were of gold. Two Angels, fifteen feet high, with wings that touched the ceiling, were covered in pure gold as well.

It took seven years for the temple to be built. Then Solomon had all his father's things, which had been dedicated to the Lord, brought into the temple. He called together the older members of the children of Israel and all the heads of the tribes and they brought in the Ark of the Lord and placed it under the wings of the Angels. Inside the Ark were the two tablets of stone that the Lord had given Moses.

Then Solomon blessed all the people. 'Blessed be the Lord God of Israel. I have built a house for the Lord and have placed the Ark which holds the Lord's laws in it inside this house. For the Lord

134

God has not failed one promise which He made to Moses. And may all the people on the earth know that the Lord *is* God and that there is none other.'

There was then a great feast which lasted seven days. On the eighth day Solomon sent the people away and they blessed him and went to their tents joyful and glad of heart for the goodness that Solomon had done and that the Lord God had done for Solomon and his people.

•

I Kings 10

The Queen of Sheba

Solomon married the Pharaoh's daughter and he built her a beautiful house. He made peace with all the neighbouring countries and brought many strangers into Israel. His fame spread very far; as far as to the Queen of Sheba. When she heard of Solomon's wisdom she came from her country to see him and find out if, indeed, he was so wise.

She came to Jerusalem with very many attendants, with camels that bore spices and much gold and precious stones. She went straight to Solomon to ask him questions, but Solomon already knew the questions she would ask and he told her all that was in her heart. When the Queen of Sheba heard this and saw the temple that Solomon had built she knew he walked with God and was truly wise.

Then she ate with the king. 'I did not believe you were wise,' she told Solomon, 'until I came here and saw for myself. Now I believe you are twice as wise as any report I received concerning your wisdom. Bless the Lord for placing you on the throne of Israel to carry out fair justice.'

Then she gave the king much gold and spices and precious stones. Never before had so many wonderful spices been brought to Israel. And King Solomon gave the Queen of Sheba all she asked for and told her all she wanted to know.

Then the Queen of Sheba departed and afterwards King Solomon made a throne of ivory covered in gold. The throne had six steps and the top of the throne was round and two lions held the throne up and twelve lions stood on each side of the six steps. There was nothing like it in any other kingdom.

So King Solomon exceeded all the kings of the earth for riches and wisdom and all the earth sought him to hear the wisdom which God had put in his heart. When they came, they brought him presents. Each year the presents grew in size. And Solomon gave freely to his people, so that everyone prospered.

•

I Kings 11–14

Solomon's Wives

King Solomon loved many strange women, together with the daughter of the Pharaoh. This did not please the Lord, for He was sure that they could turn Solomon away to worship their own gods. And at last Solomon had seven hundred wives, and they turned his heart to their gods. Now, when Solomon grew old he was worshipping his wives' gods and the Lord God grew very angry.

God then commanded Solomon *not* to worship any other god, but Solomon did not heed the Lord God's commandment.

'You have not kept your vow,' God told Solomon, 'but for your father, David, I would take the kingdom from you. But the kingdom will not pass to any of your sons. However, for David's sake, I will give one of your sons the rule of one tribe of the children of Israel.'

And when Solomon died God did as He said He would. Solomon was buried in the city of David where his father was buried. Solomon's son, Rehoboam, ruled one tribe, Judah, but Israel was ruled by Jeroboam and there were wars between the two all their days. And when each king died he was succeeded by his son.

There were many kings that followed and Israel was then divided into two parts: the north was the kingdom of Israel and the south was the kingdom of Judah. Ahab was now the king of Israel and his wife was named Jezebel, and Ahab built a temple to a false god and Elijah, the prophet, turned against him.

•

I Kings 17

Elijah and the Ravens

The priest, Elijah, said to Ahab after Ahab had built a temple to a false god, 'As the Lord God of Israel lives there shall not be rain or dew in the land!'

Then the Lord God spoke to Elijah, saying, 'Go; turn eastward and hide by the brook, Cherith. You shall drink from this brook and I have commanded the ravens to feed you there.'

So Elijah went to the brook and drank there and the ravens brought him bread and meat in the morning and bread and meat in the evening. But soon the brook dried up because there had been no rain

in the land.

God spoke to Elijah again, 'Go to Zarephath and live there. I have commanded a widow there to feed you.'

So Elijah went to Zarephath and when he came to the gate of the city a widow was there gathering sticks and Elijah called to her, 'Fetch me, I pray you, a little water to drink.' And as she was going to do so he called to her again, 'Bring me, I pray you, some bread as well.'

'I have no bread,' she told him. 'Only a

handful of meal in a barrel and a little oil in a jar.'

'Do as I say,' Elijah told her. 'Make the meal and oil into a small cake for me and then make still more for you and your son, for the Lord God will see that the barrel never empties and the jar remains the same until the Lord sends rain to our land.'

The widow did as Elijah told her and behold! the barrel did not empty and the jar remained the same!

•

I Kings 17

The Widow's Son

During the long time Elijah stayed with the widow and her small son the son grew very sick and the widow came to Elijah. 'What have I done wrong?' she asked him, 'that my son should become so sick? He will surely die.'

'Give me your son,' Elijah told her. Then he took the child from her arms and carried him up to his own room and laid the child on his own bed. Then he cried to the Lord: 'O Lord, my God, have You done this thing? If so, I beg You to make the child well again.'

The Lord God heard Elijah and the child grew pink and healthy again. Then Elijah took the child back to his mother and said, 'See, your son is well.'

'Now I know you are a man of God,' she told him, 'and that everything you say is the word of God.'

•

I Kings 18

Elijah Meets Obadiah

After many days the Lord came to Elijah. 'Go to Ahab and I will send rain on the earth.'

So Elijah went on his way to see Ahab.

At this time Ahab had called his steward Obadiah, to him.

(*Now Obadiah feared the Lord and was a good man and when Jezebel ordered all the prophets to be killed, Obadiah had taken one hundred of them and hid them in a cave and fed them bread and water.*)

'Go into the country,' said Ahab to Obadiah, 'and find grass so that our animals will not die.'

Obadiah met Elijah on his way. Obadiah fell on his knees. 'Are you not my lord Elijah?' he asked.

'I am,' Elijah told him. 'Now rise and tell Ahab I want to see him.'

'He will kill me! He has the whole nation searching for you and they have told him they could not find you. Now if I go to him and say "Elijah wants to see you" he will come immediately, and if he cannot find you, he will kill me in your stead!'

137

'I will be where Ahab can find me,' Elijah told him.

And Obadiah brought Ahab to see Elijah.

•

I Kings 18

Elijah's Sign

When Ahab met Elijah he said, 'It is you who has caused Israel so much trouble.'

'Oh, no! It is you!' Elijah told him. 'For you have not followed the Lord but a false god, Baal. Now call all the people of Israel to Mount Carmel and I will show you which is the true God!'

Ahab gathered the people on Mount Carmel and Elijah spoke to them. 'I am the only prophet of the Lord still alive but Baal's prophets are four hundred and fifty. Therefore, give us two oxen ready to be cooked. Place one on wood with no fire under it. Then let the prophets of Baal call on their god to make the fire light.'

The prophets of Baal cried and leapt up and down from morning till night but the fire did not light.

Then Elijah mocked them. 'If Baal is a god,' he said, 'he must be sleeping or on a journey!'

Elijah then took twelve stones for the twelve tribes of the sons of Jacob. With the stones he made an altar in the name of the Lord. He made a trench around the altar and put the wood in the trench. Then he cut the ox into pieces and laid the pieces on the wood. Then he told the people, 'Fill four barrels with water and pour it on the ox and the wood.' And the people did that. 'Do it a second time,' he said. And they did. 'And a third,' and they did and the water now overflowed the trench.

Then Elijah spoke to God, 'Let it be known,' he said, 'that You are the Lord God of Israel.'

And fire then leapt from the damp wood and burnt the meat and licked up all the water that was in the trench and the people fell on their faces and cried, 'The Lord *He* is the God!'

Then the skies grew black with clouds and there was a great rain.

•

I Kings 21

Naboth's Vineyard

Bordering the palace grounds of King Ahab and Jezebel, his wife, was a vineyard owned by a man named Naboth. Ahab wanted this vineyard in which to grow special herbs. He wrote to Naboth and offered him either a better vineyard or more money than the vineyard was worth. But it was Naboth's inheritence, held in his family for many years, and he refused to sell it to the king.

Ahab was very unhappy because he had had his heart set on the vineyard. When he returned to his palace he went to his room and remained there without caring to eat. Jezebel came to him there.

'Why are you so unhappy?' she asked.

'Because I spoke to Naboth and offered him another vineyard and more money than his vineyard is worth but he won't sell it to me,' the king told his wife.

'Are you not king of Israel?' Jezebel chided him. 'Arise and eat! I will go and get the vineyard for you!'

Then she left him and set to work to write two letters in Ahab's name and sealed them with Ahab's seal and sent them to two noblemen living in the city. 'Proclaim a fast,' the letters said, 'and bring Naboth before the people. Then let two young men come forward to say to Naboth, "You spoke against your God and king!" Then carry Naboth out and stone him that he may die!'

The two men did as the letters told them and the people killed Naboth. Then they sent a messenger to Jezebel saying, 'Naboth is dead.'

When Jezebel heard that Naboth was dead she told Ahab to go to Naboth's vineyard and take it. But God had spoken to Elijah, saying, 'Go down to meet Ahab, the king of Israel, in the vineyard of Naboth and speak to him saying, "The Lord says you have killed and stolen the man's land. You shall die in the same place and way that Naboth did".'

Elijah went to the vineyard and there he saw Ahab. 'It seems my enemy has found me!' Ahab said.

Elijah replied, 'Because you have done evil in the eyes of the Lord, so evil will come to you. All you have shall be taken away from you and Jezebel shall die as she ordered Naboth to die.'

Then Ahab dropped to the earth and begged forgiveness of the Lord. He lay there a long while and neither ate nor drank and then the Lord spoke to Elijah, 'Because he has humbled himself I will not bring evil to him during his lifetime.' But Jezebel died exactly as she had ordered Naboth to die.

SECOND BOOK OF KINGS

Fire on the Mountain

After the death of Ahab his son, Ahaziah, ruled over Israel. During the early part of the his reign he became very sick, and so he sent messengers to the false gods and their prophets to ask if he would recover, but his messengers met Elijah while on their way and Elijah told them, 'Because the king sent messengers to false gods he will not rise from his bed.'

The messengers went back to the king and told him what Elijah had said, and the king was very angry and sent a captain and fifty men to get Elijah and bring him back. They found Elijah on the top of a mountain and as they approached and called for him to come down, Elijah said, 'I am a man of God and God shall send down a fire and consume you!'

As he spoke a fire came down from heaven and the captain and all his men were consumed in it. Still, the king was not satisfied. He sent another captain and fifty more men and they also found Elijah on top of the mountain and ordered him to come down. The fire of God came down a second time and consumed the captain and all fifty of his men. Still the king was not satisfied! He sent another captain and fifty more men, but when this captain came near Elijah he fell to his knees. 'O man of the Lord,' he said to Elijah, 'let these fifty men in my charge be precious in your sight.'

And the Angel of the Lord told Elijah, 'Go with him. Do not be afraid.' Elijah went down the mountain with him and to the king and then Elijah told the king he would die because he did not believe in the Lord, and the king never again rose from his bed.

•

The Chariot of Fire

Elijah grew very old and he knew his days on earth were numbered, so he took Elisha with him to the place from whence he knew he would go up to heaven.

When they reached the river Jordan Elijah removed his robe and bundled it up and hit the water with it. When he did, the waters parted and he and Elisha walked to the other side. Elijah then asked Elisha, 'Tell me what I can do for you before I am taken away.'

'Give me a double portion of your spirit,' Elisha asked of him.

'That is a hard thing. Nevertheless, it shall be so,' Elijah told him.

Then, behold! There appeared a chariot of fire and horses of fire and Elijah got inside unharmed and a huge wind came up, a whirlwind, and carried Elijah up to the heavens.

Then Elisha took Elijah's robes and went back to the river Jordan and struck the waters with the robe as Elijah had done and they parted for him to return to the city. On his way he met some men

and they told him that there was no water
and the land was dry and parched.

'Bring me some salt,' Elisha told them.

They brought Elisha salt and he
poured it into the springs and there was
water from that time on. And the land
was rich with life.

•

II Kings 4

The Widow and the Oil

A widow who had been the wife of one of
the prophet's sons came to Elisha and she
was very upset. 'You know I have always
followed the word of the Lord and now a
man to whom I owe a debt has come to
take my two sons to serve him as slaves in
payment of the debt. What shall I do?'

'What have you in the house?' asked
Elisha.

'Only a pot of oil,' she replied.

'Then borrow jars from all your neighbours, as many as you can. Fill one from
the pot of oil. Soon all will be filled and
the oil will not run out,' Elisha told her.

So she went back to her house and did
as Elisha told her, and it was as he said.
The pot of oil did not empty until all the
jars were filled. Afterwards, she came to
tell Elisha.

'Now, sell the oil and pay the debt and
you will never know debt again,' he said,
and it happened as Elisha said it would.

•

II Kings 5

The Leper and the Gold

The captain of the armies of Syria was a
great and honourable man, but he

became ill with leprosy. His wife had a
maid who had been taken captive during
a war with Israel. She told her mistress
about Elisha and that he could cure her
husband of his leprosy.

The wife then went to the king of Syria
and told him what the maid had said.
The king gave her six thousand pieces of
gold for her husband to give to whoever
could cure him.

When the man arrived, the king of
Israel did not know what to do. So he
sent the man to Elisha. Elisha told the
man to go to the river Jordan and wash

himself seven times and he would be cured. But the leper was furious, for he could not believe that the waters of the Jordan would heal him better than his own rivers on Damascus. But his servants spoke to him. 'If the prophet asks you to do this,' they said, 'and you are already here, how can it harm you to do as he says?'

So the man went down and dipped himself seven times into the Jordan – and he was cured of his leprosy!

Then he came to Elisha and said, 'Now I know there is no God on earth but the God of Israel.'

He offered Elisha all the gold he had brought but Elisha refused it. Then the man went on his way. But Elisha's servant had seen the gold and he went after the man and told him that his master, Elisha, had changed his mind, which was a lie. The man gave him the gold. When the servant returned to Elisha, Elisha knew what he had done and he cast him out. And lo! the Syrian's leprosy was now upon Elisha's greedy servant!

•

for six years during which time Athaliah ruled. In the seventh year, the child was brought forward and made the rightful king. The people gathered at the temple and shouted, 'God save the king!'

When Queen Athaliah heard the people shout she came to the Temple of the Lord. There she saw the little king and heard the sound of trumpets and the rejoicing of the people and she cried, 'Treason! Treason!'

But Jehoida, the priest, told the captains of the people, 'Make her leave. Anyone who follows her will be killed.'

The men cast the queen out and no one did follow her, and Jehoash was only seven years old when he began to reign.

•

II Kings 11

The Little King

There followed many wars in Israel. Many kings died. When one battle was lost and when Athaliah, who was then the queen mother, found that her son, Ahaziah, had been killed, she herself killed all the other princes in the land so that she could rule. But her daughter took one of Ahaziah's sons and hid him and he was not slain.

The child's name was Jehoash and he was hidden in the Temple of the Lord

II Kings 13

Jehoash's Arrows

Elisha grew old during Jehoash's reign and when he was on his death-bed he called Jehoash to him.

'Take a bow and arrows,' he told him. Jehoash did as Elisha commanded. 'Now put your hand on the bow.' Jehoash did this. Elisha placed his hands over the king's hands. 'Open the window to the east,' Elisha said. The king opened the window. 'Shoot,' Elisha told him.

The king shot and the arrow went through the window. 'That is the arrow of the Lord's deliverance,' Elisha told him. 'You will fight the Syrians until you have won.'

Then Elisha joined his fathers.

Josiah's Good Reign

The little king had many problems and other men took the kingdom from him. There were cruel times until another child became king. His name was Josiah. He was only eight years old when he was crowned king. He grew up to be a very good king and he kept the Lord's laws. He had destroyed all the false gods of the people by the time he was eighteen. Then he held a solemn passover and there had not been such a passover held since the time of Moses and there had been none like Josiah since Moses. Josiah fought many brave battles and was killed fighting for the Lord and the people brought him back to Jerusalem in a chariot and buried him there.

And then other kings ruled and evil came back into the land, and other countries took over Israel. And then Jerusalem fell and was taken.

EZRA·NEHEMIAH and ESTHER

Ezra 7–10

Nehemiah 1–6

The Story of Ezra

Ezra was a man of God and a writer as well. He studied the law of the Lord and the king commanded him to set up magistrates and judges to judge all the people and to teach them many things. But the princes of the land came to Ezra and told him that the people of Israel had taken strangers from other lands for their wives, who turned their husbands away from the Lord God and to their heathen gods.

Ezra then fell on his knees and spread out his hands to the Lord and said, 'O my Lord! False gods are now making our land unclean. Give us a wall in Judah and in Jerusalem, O Lord, so that we may keep these false gods out of Israel and Judah.'

When Ezra had finished praying and confessing, a very great congregation of men and women and children came to him and they wept with him. But they said when they looked at Ezra., 'We have sinned against our God and have taken strange wives, yet there is still hope. We will make a vow and cast out all the wives who worship false idols and the children they have borne. And Ezra, please be with us, for you are a man of courage and a man of the Lord.'

Rebuilding the Wall

Nehemiah went to the king of Persia and the king saw that Nehemiah was very sad.

'Why are you so unhappy?' he asked him.

'Because the city of Jerusalem, where my own father is buried, lies in waste,' Nehemiah replied.

'What can I do for you?' the king asked.

'If it please the king to send me to Jerusalem that I might rebuild it,' Nehemiah replied.

'How long shall you take and when will you return?' the king asked.

Nehemiah gave him a time and the king agreed. Then Nehemiah arose in the night and, taking a few men with him and little else, went out through the valley and to the gate and the broken walls of Jerusalem. Then Nehemiah told the people of the king's word and the people rose up to rebuild the wall of the city of Jerusalem.

The work was divided among the different men of the different tribes, and it was begun. But the Arabians and the Ammonites heard that the wall was being rebuilt so they plotted to destroy it again. Then Nehemiah divided his men into two parties: half guarded the wall while the others worked and the ones who watched stood with their bows ready. Even the builders had swords by their sides.

For forty-two days the men did not take off their clothes as they stood watch and rebuilt the wall. Finally, it was whole once again.

•

Nehemiah 7–13

The Dedication

When the wall was rebuilt and the doors put in place and the porters and the singers and the priests had been chosen, Nehemiah appointed his brother, Hanani, ruler of the palace and in charge of Jerusalem because he was a faithful man and feared God.

Nehemiah told the people, 'Do not open the gates of Jerusalem while the enemy is close. Shut the doors and bar them; appoint men to watch the wall and guard their own houses.'

Now the city was large and the houses had not all been rebuilt. So the officials lived in Jerusalem and the rest of the people cast lots for the houses that remained.

And at the dedication of the wall there was much gladness and singing with cymbals and harps. The sons of the singers gathered together and built villages around Jerusalem and the priests purified the people and the gates and the wall. And then Nehemiah prayed to the Lord to remember him.

•

The Story of Esther

Ahasuerus, the king of the Persians, ruled one hundred and twenty-seven provinces in India and Ethiopia. He gave a big feast and all his nobles and princes from all the provinces were present. The feast lasted seven days and the palace was magnificently decorated.

At the same time Vashti, the queen, gave a feast for all the women of the royal house. Now, on the seventh day of the king's feast, when he was merry with drink, he called his seven chambermaids and ordered them to fetch Queen Vashti so that he could show off her great beauty to all the nobles and princes. But the queen refused to obey the king's command and the king grew very angry.

Then King Ahasuerus turned to his wise men and asked, 'What shall we do with Queen Vashti because she has disobeyed the king's command?'

'If it please the king, let there be a royal commandment and let it be written among the laws of the Persians that Queen Vashti should come no more before the king and let the king give her royal estate to another.'

So a proclamation went out to find a beautiful young girl to wed the king. And officers were appointed in all the provinces to look for this girl.

Now there was a Jew named Mordecai who had raised his dead uncle's daughter, Esther, as if she were his own. She was very beautiful. So when the king's officers brought all the beautiful girls before the king, Esther was among them, and it was Esther who pleased him the most. The king did not know that she was a Jewess. He gave her the best rooms and he loved her above all the other women in the palace and he set the royal crown upon her head and made her queen in Vashti's place. Then he made a great feast in Esther's honour. Still Esther did not tell the king, nor did Mordecai, that she was a Jewess.

And it came to pass that a large sum of money was raised by the king's treasuries to destroy all the Jews.

Mordecai sent a messenger to Queen Esther to tell her she should now go to the king and declare herself a Jewess and

beg the king to save her people. But Esther was afraid. So Mordecai sent her another message telling her she was foolish to think she would be spared above the rest of the Jews.

Esther sent Mordecai this answer: 'Gather together all the Jews in the city and fast for three days and three nights and I and my handmaidens shall fast as well. Then I will go to the king and, if I am to die, then I shall die a Jewess.'

On the third day of the fast, Esther put on her royal robes and came before the king on his throne. The king was so moved by her beauty that he came down from his throne with his golden sceptre and said to her, 'Whatever you want I will give you.'

'I would like you to come to a banquet that I have prepared for you,' she said.

And the king came to the banquet and again asked Esther, 'What can I do for you? Whatever you want you shall have.'

'I want you to come again to dinner with your servant Haman,' she said. (*Haman was the man who was to destroy the Jews.*)

Haman went home and told his wife he had been invited to a dinner Queen Esther was giving and that no other men except the king and himself would be there. He was very pleased. So the king and Haman went to the banquet with Esther the queen. And the king said to her again, 'What can I do for you? Whatever you ask you shall have.'

'If it please my lord, let my life and the lives of my people be spared because I am a Jewess and I have held my tongue, but now my people have been sold and I, with them, am to be destroyed.'

'Who has done this thing?' the king asked.

'Haman,' Esther said, looking at him.

And Haman was afraid before the king and queen. And the king rose from the dinner table in fury and then Haman begged Esther that his life be spared. But the king had Haman put to death.

The king struck out the order given by Haman and honoured Mordecai by putting him in Haman's place. And the Jews had light and gladness and joy, and many people of the kingdom who were not Jews became Jews, for Mordecai was next to the king and Esther the queen was beloved by him.

JOB

Satan Tempts Job

There was a man in the land of Uz whose name was Job and that man was perfect and upright and one who feared God and hated evil, and he had seven sons and three daughters. Now there came a day when the sons of God presented themselves to the Lord and Satan came with them.

'Why do you come here?' the Lord asked Satan.

'Because I believe there is evil in every man,' Satan told Him.

'Have you not seen My servant, Job? He is a perfect man and follows good in every way,' the Lord told Satan.

'Job has everything,' Satan told Him. 'Take away some of these things and then see how perfect he is.'

Well, one day when Job and his family were feasting, a servant came in from the fields to tell him that one of his servants had been slain and his animals taken away, and before this servant could even finish, another servant ran in and said, 'The fire of God is fallen from the heavens and all you had has been burnt and I alone of all your men escaped!'

And while this man talked there came a great wind from the wilderness and the house fell in on his children. Job arose but the children were dead. He fell down upon the ground and prayed and said, 'Naked came I out of my mother's womb, and naked I shall return. The Lord gives and the Lord takes away. Blessed be the name of the Lord.'

And so Job was not tempted by Satan.

•

Satan Tempts a Second Time

Now the sons of God again came to present themselves to the Lord, and Satan came among them and the Lord said to Satan, 'Why are you here?'

'Because I believe there is evil in every man,' Satan replied.

151

'Have you not seen how good is My servant, Job? No matter what befalls him he still believes and does not move against Me.'

'Ah, skin for skin,' Satan said. 'His life has not been in danger.'

'I will place him in your hands,' God said, 'so that you can see he is perfect; but save his life.'

And Satan cursed Job with a terrible illness that caused boils to cover his body. But Job still believed in God and would not go against Him.

Then, after a time when the pain and illness did not stop and three of his friends had come to mourn with him, he could stand it no longer and cursed the day he was born. 'Let there be darkness,' he cried, 'let God's light fade and darkness and shadow and clouds and blackness settle on the earth! And as for the night, let darkness seize it so that there will be no sounds of joy in the night. Let the stars stop shining and the dawn held back!'

His three friends argued with Job and told him all the beauties of God's ways and Job told them the great unhappiness that came with following the path of God. But then God came to Job out of a whirlwind and spoke to him:

'Who is this who curses life without knowledge of what life is? Be a man now, for I will demand answers to questions. Where were you when I laid the foundations of the earth? Who made the morning stars sing and closed the doors of the sea so that there would be earth and water? What causes the light and the darkness? Why were you born? Who causes the rain and the flowers to grow? Who has given man wisdom and understanding in his heart?'

Then Job answered the Lord, 'What shall I answer You? Tell me.' And then he said, 'I know that You can do everything and that no thought can be held from You. I beg You to forgive me.'

And the Lord had mercy on Job and made his latter years better than his early ones. He became prosperous again and his wife had seven more sons and three more daughters, and Job lived to a very old age to see his great, great grandchildren. And his life was full and his praise of the Lord great.

●

PROPHETS I

Isaiah, Jeremiah (Lamentations) and Ezekiel

The First Three Prophets

The last part of the Old Testament was written by the prophets, the men who preached God's words and who told the people what might happen in the future. The first three of these, ISAIAH, JEREMIAH *(who also wrote the* Lamentations *which mourned the fall of Jerusalem) and* EZEKIEL, *all lived during and just after the fall of Jerusalem, and for the following seventy years when the children of Israel wandered again.*

The people at this time were held together and led onward by these prophets who promised them their return to Jerusalem, the end to their wandering and their wars, and also predicted that a man of God, like Moses, would be born to lead them to bring the Gentiles and the Jews together. Isaiah says it this way:

'But in the end it will come to pass
That the House of the Lord shall be established
On the top of the mountains;
And many people and nations shall come and say,
"Come, let us go up to the mountain of the Lord,
And to the House of the God of Jacob,
And He will teach us His ways
And we will walk in His paths,
For the law shall go forth from Zion
And the word of the Lord from Jerusalem
And He shall judge among many people.

And they shall turn their swords into plows
And their spears into pruning forks.
Nation shall not lift up a sword against nation.
And they shall fight no more wars." '

DANIEL

The Four Princes

Daniel was born when Jerusalem fell, and his people, the children of Israel, were in exile and wandering again. Nebuchadnezzar, the king of Babylon, had captured the city. Now, he gave an order that some of Israel's young princes should remain as hostages. He chose only those who were healthy, handsome and very bright. These princes ate and slept in the king's house. They were to be taught the ways and the language of the king, and at the end of three years they were to be brought before King Nebuchadnezzar.

Daniel was one of these princes. There were three others and their names were Shadrach, Meshach, and Abednego. Of the four boys, the king favoured Daniel the most, so when Daniel told the master of the king's household that he would not eat the king's meat, the man was very worried.

'If the king sees your face paler and thinner than any of the other children in the palace, he will turn his anger on me!' he told Daniel.

'Give us ten days,' the four princes said, 'and we will show you that we won't become thin and pale without the king's meat. Let us eat only vegetables and give us only water to drink for those ten days,' Daniel added.

The master of the household agreed to this and gave the four princes only water

to drink and vegetables to eat and after the ten days their faces were rosier and fatter than those of the children who had eaten the king's meat and drunk the king's wine. After that they were never made to eat the meat and so they did not go against the law of the Lord that forbade them to eat such unholy food.

•

Daniel Tells the King's Dream

During the second year of Daniel's captivity, the king had a dream and he awoke, troubled and frightened; but he could not remember the dream once he was awake. He called in all his wise men and astrologers and commanded them to tell him what he had dreamt and what the dream meant.

'If you can tell *us* what you dreamt we will interpret it for you, but no one can tell *you* what the dream *was*,' they told him.

The king was angry and he ordered them all to be killed. Now Daniel heard of this order and he asked to see the king and was given an audience.

'Don't kill the wise men and the astrologers,' Daniel told the king. 'I will tell you what your dream was about for there is a God in Heaven Who reveals secrets. He made your dream known to me so that these innocent men could be saved

will establish a kingdom that will stand for ever.'

The king then fell to his knees and bowed to Daniel, for Daniel had told him what he had dreamed. Then the king made Daniel a great man, gave him many gifts and made him ruler over a part of the country. And he also made the three other princes, Shadrach, Meshach, and Abednego, sit in judgment as wise men.

•

Daniel 3

Shadrach, Meshach and Abednego

and so you would know God's wisdom. You saw a great image, and it was so large and so glaring that it was terrible. The head was of gold, the breasts and arms of silver, the belly and thighs of brass, the legs of iron, but the feet were of clay. Then a stone smashed the feet of clay to bits and the rest of the giant statue fell and crumbled into such small pieces that when a wind came they were carried away. But the stone that smashed the statue's clay feet became a great mountain and filled the whole earth.' Then Daniel told the king what the dream meant. 'You are a king of strength and glory. You *are* the head of gold. But after you there shall be another kingdom, not as good as yours; a third kingdom of brass; and the fourth kingdom shall be as strong as iron, but it shall break into pieces. And, as you saw the feet of clay crumble, so shall that kingdom crumble and then intermingle with all the other nations on the earth and so disappear. When that happens, the God in heaven

Now the King of Babylon had a great statue ninety feet tall made of gold and he issued a decree that all his people,

whenever they heard the sound of certain music, should fall down and worship the golden image and whosoever did not would be thrown into a fiery furnace. But the three princes, Shadrach, Meshach, and Abednego, would not follow the decree and they were brought before the king.

The music was then played for them but they still would not fall to their knees and worship a false god, so the king, in a terrible anger, ordered the fiery furnace to be made seven times hotter than usual and Shadrach, Meshach, and Abednego, with all their clothes on, were thrown into it. But when the king looked into the fire, Shadrach, Meshach, and Abednego were dancing in the flames with a fourth person.

'They are unhurt!' the king exclaimed. 'And the son of God is with them!'

Then the three princes came out of the fiery furnace and they *were* unhurt; not one hair was singed on their heads, nor did they have the smell of the fire on their clothes.

Then the king said, 'Blessed be the God of Shadrach, Meshach, and Abednego, for He has saved them from a fiery death because they would not worship another god.'

The king rewarded the three princes and issued another decree that no one should say anything against *their* God.

•

Daniel 4

The King's Second Dream

The king dreamed a second dream and again it was so terrible he could not remember it when he awoke, so he called for Daniel.

'You dreamed there was a tree in the centre of the earth,' Daniel told him. 'And it was so tall that it touched the heaven and there was enough fruit on it to feed every living thing. Then a holy one came down from heaven and cried, "Cut down the tree, cut off the branches, shake off the leaves, and scatter the fruit; but leave the stump and the roots, and man's heart shall be changed to that of a beast!"' Then Daniel looked troubled. 'The dream, O king, is about those who hate you and are your enemies. The tree is you, O king, tall and strong: but your enemies will destroy most of your kingdom. Still, your roots shall remain – but you will live like an animal until, after a certain time, you will become strong again. For you will know then that the Lord in the heavens rules, not you.'

And it all came to pass as Daniel said it would.

•

The Writing on the Wall

King Nebuchadnezzar died and his son, Belshazzar, became king; and when he did he held a great feast for one thousand of his lords. He took all the golden goblets that had been in the temple of the Lord and served his guests wine in them and as they drank, lo! the fingers of a man's hand appeared in space and then moved and wrote upon the wall. The king was so frightend that his knees knocked together!

But he could not read what the hand had written and so he called out, 'Whoever reads this writing and tells me what it means shall be clothed in scarlet and have a chain of gold about his neck and shall be the third in this kingdom in line of rule.'

All the king's wise men came in but they could not read what the hand had written. Then the queen spoke and told the king of Daniel and the king remembered Daniel and had him brought into the great banqueting hall.

This is what Daniel told the king: 'O king, the most high God gave your father a kingdom and majesty and glory and honour, and so all nations and people followed him. But when he went against God, all this was taken away from him and he lived like an animal until he knew the high God ruled in the kingdom of men. Now you, his son, have gone against the high God. You have taken holy goblets from His temple and drunk wine from them and you have set up idols of gold and silver and brass and iron and wood and stone, which see not, nor hear, nor know. And to the *true* God who holds your life in His hands, you have given nothing. So this is the writing that was written: *Mene, Mene, Tekel, Upharsin*. And this is what it means: *Mene*, God has numbered the days of your reign and ended it. *Tekel*: You have been weighed in the scales and found wanting. *Upharsin*: Your kingdom has been divided and given half to the Medes and half to the Persians.'

The king had Daniel clothed in scarlet and placed a gold chain around his neck and issued a proclamation making him third ruler in the kingdom. But that very same night King Belshazzar was killed and Darius, who was a Mede, became king.

●

Daniel in the Lion's Den

King Darius was very pleased with Daniel. He made him president over the kingdom of one hundred and twenty princes and all the princes had to come to him for approval. This made them unhappy and they tried to find some fault with Daniel but they could not. Then they plotted against him. They made a law that they presented to King Darius ordering anyone who asked anything of any god or man except the king for thirty days should be cast into a den of lions.

King Darius signed the order. Daniel knew of the order, but he still went to his house and opened his windows facing the city, and kneeled and prayed and gave thanks to his God, as he always did three times a day.

The princes saw him and went immediately to the king. 'Did you not sign an order that anyone who asked anything of any god for thirty days, except yourself, should be thrown into a den of lions?' they asked.

'I did,' the king replied.

'Daniel does not respect you, for he prays to his God three times a day,' the princes told the king. When the king heard this he was terribly unhappy and he set his heart on saving Daniel. He thought all day about how to save Daniel. Then when the princes came to him again he told them to send Daniel into the lions' den. Then he told Daniel, 'Your God will save you.'

The king went to his palace and fasted the whole night and he did not sleep. Very early the next morning the king hurried to the den of the lions. Daniel was there, unharmed. The king was much relieved.

'My God has sent His Angel to shut the lions' mouths so they would not hurt me,' Daniel told him.

The king then commanded that Daniel be brought up out of the den. And after that Daniel lived well during the reign of King Darius.

PROPHETS II

A Warning from the Prophets

(There were then four more prophets in the Old Testament who warned the children of Israel of the fall of their nations. These were HOSEA, JOEL, AMOS and OBADIAH. Joel warned the people):

There will come a day of darkness and gloom
And a great and strong people
Like the noise of chariots shall they leap.
They shall run like mighty men,
They shall climb the wall like men of war.

They shall march every one on his way
And they shall not break ranks.
They shall attack the city.
They shall climb up upon the houses.
They shall enter the windows like a thief.
The earth shall quake.
The heavens shall tremble.
The sun and the moon shall be dark.
And the stars shall not shine.

JONAH

Jonah 1–4

Jonah and the Whale

Now the word of the Lord came to Jonah and said to him, 'Go to Nineveh and stand up against the people of that great city, for they are going into the paths of wickedness.'

But Jonah did not do as the Lord told him; instead he went down to Joppa where he found a ship going to Tarshish,

160

and he paid his fare and he went aboard and the ship sailed for Tarshish.

The Lord then sent a great wind into the sea and there was a mighty tempest and the ship was nearly wrecked. All the sailors were afraid and they all cried to their own gods and threw things into the sea from the ship to lighten the load. But Jonah, during this great storm, lay fast asleep down in his cabin.

The master of the ship came to him. 'Why are you sleeping?' he asked. 'Call on your God to help us, and if He wills it, maybe we will not die.'

Then all the sailors gathered. 'Come let us cast lots,' they said, 'so that we will know who it is who caused this terrible thing.' So they cast lots and the lot fell upon Jonah.

They came to Jonah. 'Tell us,' they asked, 'where do you come from and what do you do? What is your country? Who are your people?'

'I am a Hebrew,' he said, 'and I fear the Lord, the God of Heaven who has made the sea and the land.' Then he told them what God had asked him to do and how he had gone against His word and come on this ship to Tarshish.

The men were frightened. 'What shall we do to calm the sea that your God has made angry at us?' they asked.

'Take me,' Jonah told them, 'and throw me into the sea and then the sea shall be calm because I know it is I who has caused this great tempest.'

Nevertheless, the men kept Jonah aboard and rowed hard to bring it to shore, but they could not for the sea grew even worse and though they did not want to do so for fear of having a man's death on their conscience, they grew more frightened and so they lifted Jonah and tossed him into the sea. As soon as they had done so the sea became calm again and the men offered the Lord their prayers.

Now the Lord had prepared a giant whale to swallow Jonah and Jonah was in the whale's belly for three days. Jonah prayed to the Lord from the whale's belly and the Lord heard him and spoke to the whale and the whale spat Jonah out of his belly and on to dry land.

Then the word of the Lord came to Jonah the second time, saying, 'Go to Nineveh, that great city, and preach what I tell you to preach.'

So this time Jonah went to Nineveh and, when he got there, the first thing he cried to the people was: 'Forty days and Nineveh shall be overthrown!' The people, from the greatest to the smallest, believed him and stopped their wickedness.

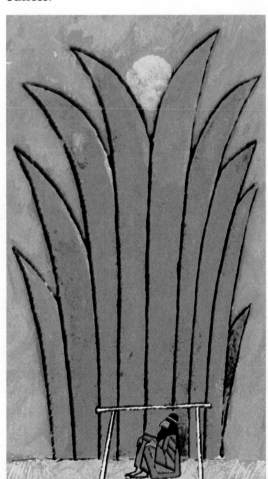

God saw what they did and so they were left in peace. Now this displeased Jonah exceedingly and he was very angry and he said to the Lord, 'Was not this what I said when I ran from You before? I knew You were a merciful God. Yet You followed me. Therefore, O Lord, take my life, for it is better for me to die than live.'

'Do you think you have that right?' the Lord asked.

Jonah could not reply, so he went out of the city and sat on the east side of the city and there he made a small shelter from the sun and sat under it to see what would become of the city. Then God made a giant plant sprout up over the shelter so it was cool inside and Jonah was very glad the plant was there. But by the next morning God had had a worm eat into the plant and the plant withered and died. Then God caused a strong east wind and the sun beat down on Jonah's head until he nearly fainted and *wished* himself dead. Then God said to Jonah, 'Do you think you still have the right to be angry?'

'I have the right to be angry until I die,' Jonah replied, 'when a plant can die so easily.'

Then the Lord said, 'You have pity on a plant which you did not nurture or make grow and which came up in one night and died in the same time. Then should I not spare Nineveh, that great city with one hundred and twenty thousand people?'

•

THE PROPHECY

Micah, Nahum, Habakkuk, Zephaniah, Haggai, Zechariah and Malachi

(*After Jonah there were the prophets* MICAH, NAHUM, HABAKKUK, ZEPHANIAH, HAGGAI, ZECHARIAH, *and* MALACHI, *and they all preached of a time when all nations would be at peace and worship the Lord in that peace. It is said here by the prophet* ZECHARIAH):

I lifted up my eyes again and looked
And behold! There was a man with a measuring tape in his hand.
'Where are you going?' I asked.
'To measure the city of Jerusalem,' he said.
But then an Angel went to meet him.
'Jerusalem shall be a city without walls,'
The Angel said, 'For the Lord will be her wall and glory,
And many nations shall be joined to the Lord
And be His people.'

And MICAH said:
'The Lord only requires you to do just, love mercy, and walk humbly with your God.'

'Before you weary of the Lord
He will give you a sign.
A virgin shall bear a son
And shall call his name Immanuel.
Butter and honey shall he eat.
That he may know to refuse evil and choose good.'

ISAIAH

163

BOOK OF PSALMS

PSALM 8

(A psalm of David to the chief musician.)
O Lord, how great is your name in all the
earth!
For you have set your glory above the
heavens.
Out of the mouths of babes you have sent
wisdom
And your might has stilled the enemy.
When I consider your heavens
The work of your fingers,
The moon and the stars you have created
What is man that you are aware of him?
And the son of man that you have visited
him?
For you have made him a little lower than
the angels
And have crowned him with glory and
honour
You made him master of things of your
making
And put all things under his feet:
All sheep and oxen, yes, and beasts of the
field,
The birds in the air and the fish of the
sea.
O Lord, how great is your name on the
earth!

PSALM 23

(A psalm of David)
The Lord is my shepherd, I shall not
want.
He makes me lie down in green pastures,
He leads me beside the still waters.
He restores my soul:
He leads me in the paths of righteousness
for His name's sake.
Yes, though I walk through the valley of
the shadow of death,
I will fear no evil:
For He is with me.
His rod and His staff they comfort me.
He prepares a table before me in the
presence of my enemies:
He anoints my head with oil; my cup
runs over.
Surely goodness and mercy shall follow
me all the days of my life;
And I will live in the house of the Lord
for ever.

PSALM 24

The earth is the Lord's and the fulness
thereof,
The world, and they that dwell therein;
For He has founded it upon the seas,
And established it upon the floods.
Lift up your heads,
   And be lifted up,
Open your everlasting doors,
And the King of Glory shall come in.

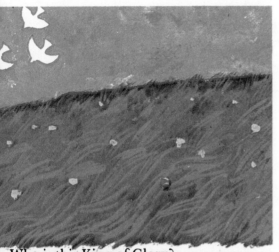

Who is this King of Glory?
The Lord, strong and mighty,
The Lord of Hosts, He is the King of Glory.

PSALM 100

(A psalm of praise)
Make a joyful noise to the Lord, all the lands.
Serve the Lord with gladness:
Come before His presence with singing.
For the Lord He *is* God:
It is He that has made us, and not we ourselves;
We are His people, and the sheep of His pasture.
Enter into His gates with thanksgiving, and into His courts with praise:
Be thankful to Him and bless His name.
For the Lord is good;
His mercy is everlasting;
And His truth endures to all generations.

•

PSALM 67

(A song)
God be merciful to us, and bless us;
And cause His face to shine upon us, amen.
That His way may be known upon earth and nations.
Let the people praise you, O God.
Let all the people praise you.
O let the nations be glad and sing for joy:
For you shall judge the people righteously,
And govern the nations on the earth, amen.
Let the people praise you, O God,
Let all the people praise you.
And God will bless us;
And all the ends of the earth shall fear Him.

•

PSALM 108

O God, my heart is fixed;
I will sing and give praise,
Even with my glory.
I will awake early.
I will praise you, O Lord, among the people
And I will sing praises to you among the nations.
For your mercy is great above the heavens:
And your truth reaches to the clouds.
Give us help from trouble:
for vain is the help of man.
Through God we shall do valiantly:
For He it is that shall tread down our enemies.

•

PROVERBS

1. A wise man will hear, and will increase his learning;
   And a man of understanding shall look for wise counsel.
2. Say not to your neighbour, 'Go and come again and tomorrow I will give you,' when you have it to give today.
3. The wise shall inherit glory, but shame shall be the portion of fools.
4. Enter not into the path of the wicked, and go not in the way of evil men. Avoid it, pass not by it, turn from it, and pass away.

5. The path of the just is a shining light, the way of the wicked is like darkness; and they know not at what they stumble.
6. A wise son makes a glad father, but a foolish son is the heaviness of his mother.
7. He that hides hatred with lying lips, and he that speaks slander, is a fool.
8. The tongue of the just is silver; the heart of the wicked is worth little.
9. The lips of the righteous feed many, but fools die for want of wisdom.
10. He that troubles his own house shall inherit the wind.
11. Pride goes before destruction and a haughty spirit before a fall.
12. Children's children are the crown of old men; and the glory of children are their fathers.
13. Love not sleep, lest you come to poverty, open your eyes, and you shall be satisfied with bread.
14. A good name is better than great riches, and loving favour better than silver and gold.
15. Train up a child in the way he should go; and when he is old, he will not depart from it.
16. Buy the truth, also wisdom and understanding and sell them not.
17. The locusts have no king, yet they go forth all in a band.
18. The spider takes hold with her hands and lives in kings' palaces.

ECCLESIASTES

Ecclesiastes 1

1. Vanity of vanities, all is vanity.
2. What profit has a man of all his labour which he takes under the sun?
3. One generation passes away and another generation comes, but the earth stays for ever.
4. The sun also rises, and the sun goes down, and hastens to the place where it arose.
5. The wind goes towards the south and turns about to the north, it whirls about continually, and the wind returns again.
6. All the rivers run into the sea; and yet the sea is not full, for where the rivers come from they return again.
7. The thing that has been is that which shall be, and that which is done is that which shall be done, and there is no new thing under the sun.
8. That which is crooked cannot be made straight; and that which is wanting cannot be numbered.

•

Ecclesiastes 2

I said of laughter, It is mad.
I made great works; I build me houses and planted me vineyards:
I made me gardens and orchards, and I planted trees in them of all kinds of fruits.
I made me pools of water, to water the wood and make the trees grow.
I got me servants and maidens.
I gathered me silver and gold.
I got me singers and songs.
So I was great.

Then I looked on all the works that my hands had wrought
And on the labour I had done,
And behold! all was vanity and there was no profit under the sun.
Then I saw that the wise man's eyes are in his head; but the fool walks in darkness.
Then I said to my heart, 'As it happens to a fool, so it happens to me.'
Then I said in my heart, 'All this is vanity.'

•

Ecclesiastes 3

To everything there is a season
And a time to every purpose under the
   heaven:
A time to be born, and a time to die;
A time to plant, and a time to pluck up
   that which is planted;
A time to kill; and a time to heal.
A time to break down, and a time to build
   up;
A time to weep, and a time to laugh;
A time to mourn, and a time to dance;
A time to cast away stones, and a time to
   gather stones together.
A time to embrace, and a time to refrain
   from embracing.
A time to get, and a time to lose;
A time to keep, and a time to cast away;
A time to rend, and a time to sew;
A time to keep silence and a time to
   speak;
A time to love, and a time to hate,
A time of war, and a time of peace.

•

Ecclesiastes 4

Two are better than one;
Because they have a good reward for
   their labour.
For if they fall, the one will lift up his
   fellow:
But woe to him that is alone when he
   falls,
For he has not another to help him up.
Again, if two lie together, then they have
   heat:
But how can one be warm alone?
And if one prevail against him,
Two shall withstand him;
And a threefold cord is not quickly
   broken.

•

SONG OF SONGS

Rise up, my love, my fair one, and come
   away,
For the winter is past, and the rain is over
   and gone;
The flowers appear on the earth;
The time of the singing of birds is come,
   and the voice of the turtle is heard in
   our land;
The fig tree puts forth her green figs,
   and the
Vines with the tender grape give a good
   smell.
Arise, my love, my fair one, and come
   away.

Take us the foxes, the little foxes
that spoil the vines; for our vines have
   tender grapes.

THE NEW TESTAMENT

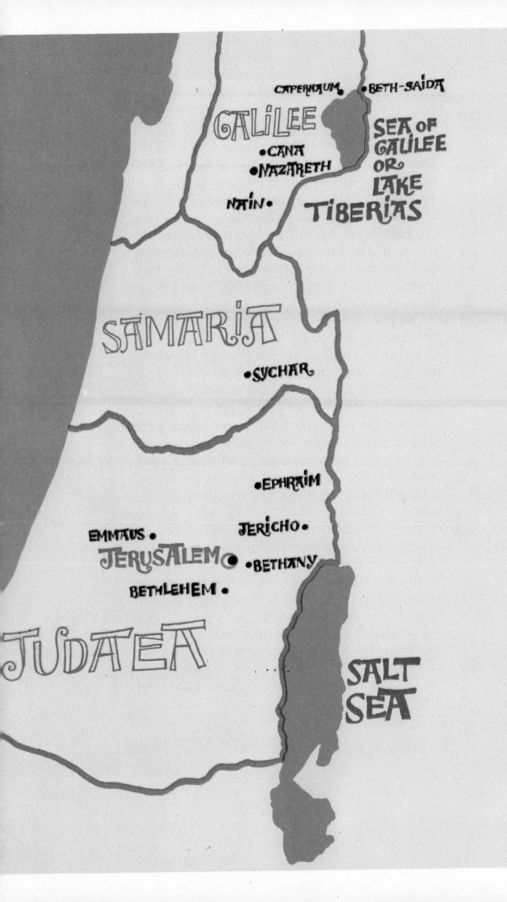

Foreword

This story takes place in Palestine nearly 2,000 years ago. Traditionally the home of the Jews, the entire country was ruled by the Romans who had conquered it many years before. The Jews felt humiliated by this and were awaiting the arrival of the Messiah, one who, according to their prophets, would be sent by God to lead the Jews against the Romans and restore the Jews to their former glory.

The Jews, who at this time lived in and around Jerusalem where they had their Temple, observed strict religious laws and looked down on non-Jews. They also despised their fellow Jews who worked for the Romans as tax collectors, and regarded those who did this job as sinners.

Within the Jewish community itself there were various groups which are frequently mentioned in the story. Pharisees, a group of devout Jews, believed in life after death; Saducees, a group of priestly Jews, very rich and very strict, did not believe in life after death; and the Chief Priests of the Temple who had enormous influence.

Herod the King (mentioned at the beginning of the story) was a Roman-appointed King. After his death a relative of his, also called Herod, was appointed Tetrarch (which meant ruler but not king) of a section of Palestine.

This abridged version of the New Testament is told in simple language for today's child and — by means of the references given on each page — can be used as a stepping stone to the authorised Bible.

CHAPTER ONE

St. Luke 1–1-56

Elisabeth and Zacharias

In the days when Herod was king of Judea, there was a priest called Zacharias who had a wife, Elisabeth. They had no children and were now very old. One day when Zacharias was in the Temple burning incense, an angel suddenly appeared before him.

Zacharias was overwhelmed, but the angel said, 'I am the angel Gabriel. Do not be afraid, Zacharias. Your prayers have been heard and your wife, Elisabeth, will bear a son. He will be one of God's men and will bring many of the people of Israel back to the Lord. And you must call him John.' Zacharias could not believe these words. 'How can this be true,' he said, 'I am an old man and my wife is well on in years.'

'I have been sent to tell you this good news,' replied the angel, 'and now you will be silent and unable to speak until your son is born – because you did not believe.'

The congregation waiting outside the Temple were astonished when Zacharias came out, and they could see that he was dumb. They realised that he had seen a vision in the Temple.

Zacharias returned home to his wife. Some weeks later she discovered that she *was* going to have a baby and she was very happy.

St. Luke 1–1-56

Mary is Chosen

Now Elisabeth had a cousin called Mary who lived in the town of Nazareth in the district of Galilee. Mary was engaged to marry a carpenter called Joseph.

One day, a few months before Elisabeth's baby was due to be born, the angel Gabriel came into the room where Mary was, and said, 'Greetings, Mary. Do not be frightened. God loves you very much. You are to have a son, and you will call him Jesus. He will be known as the Son of God and he will reign over the people of Jacob for ever.'

And Mary replied, 'How can it be that I shall have a child? I am not yet married.'

Gabriel reassured her that this was God's will and added, 'Your cousin Elisabeth, who has always been unable to have children and who is now quite old, has also conceived a son.'

Mary, convinced, said, 'I accept the Lord's wishes. I belong to the Lord.' And the angel departed.

She wasted no time in getting ready and travelled to visit Elisabeth in Jerusalem. They greeted each other and Elisabeth said, 'I am honoured that you should visit me, you who are to be the mother of my Lord.'

'I am full of praise for God, and joy,' said Mary. 'Future generations will call me the happiest woman who ever lived.' Mary stayed with Elisabeth for three months then returned to her home.

●

Joseph's Dream

When Joseph saw that Mary was pregnant, he felt obliged to break off the engagement, but quietly since he did not want her to be publicly disgraced. But whilst he was thinking it over, he had a dream in which an angel of God appeared and told him: 'Joseph, Mary has conceived through the Holy Spirit. She will give birth to a son whom you will call Jesus, which means Saviour, for he has been chosen to save the people from their sins. Do not be afraid to marry Mary.'

When Joseph awoke he did as the angel had told him. And soon afterwards he and Mary were married.

•

St. Luke 1–59-66

The Birth of John

Meanwhile Elisabeth's son was born. When he was eight days old and was to be circumcised, everyone expected that he would be named Zacharias after his father. But his mother said: 'He is to be called John.' At this everyone was very surprised and made signs to Zacharias, asking what name he wanted. Zacharias beckoned for something on which to write, and he wrote 'His name is John'.

And immediately his power of speech returned, and the first words he spoke were prayers to God. And all the people were astonished by the events and the news was recounted throughout Judea.

•

St. Luke 2–1-20

The Birth of Jesus

When it was nearly time for Mary's child to be born, a law was announced by Augustus Caesar that all the people in the world should be registered and everybody had to go to the town where they had been born for this registration to take place. Joseph and Mary went from Nazareth to Bethlehem.

Although they looked everywhere for a room to stay, the town was full so they had to sleep in a stable and here Mary's baby was born, and she wrapped him up and laid him in a manger.

Not far away there were some shepherds looking after their flocks of sheep throughout the night. And suddenly an angel appeared before them and there was a great brilliance, and the shepherds were very frightened.

And the angel said: 'Do not be afraid. I bring you wonderful news. Today in David's city a Saviour has been born for you. He is Christ the Lord. You will find him wrapped up and lying in a manger.'

At once there appeared with the angel a great throng of angels saying: 'Glory to God in Heaven and on earth peace towards men who are good.'

Then the angels left the shepherds, and the shepherds said to each other: 'Let's hurry to Bethlehem and see this thing for ourselves.'

St. Luke 2–1-20

The Shepherds' Visit

They travelled quickly and found Mary and Joseph, and the baby lying in the manger. And, having seen the baby, they told everybody what had been told to them about the child, and then returned to their work marvelling at what had happened. Mary cherished these memories in her heart.

●

St. Luke 2–21-35

Simeon's Prophecy

When he was eight days old, the baby was circumcised and named Jesus as the angel had instructed before his birth. And, on his fortieth day, he was taken to the Temple in Jerusalem in accordance with the custom of that time so that his parents could offer a sacrifice of two young pigeons or a pair of turtle doves.

There was in Jerusalem at that time, a man called Simeon who was very devout. He was old, and he had been given a sign that he should not die before he had seen the Lord's Christ.

He was in the Temple when Joseph and Mary arrived with the baby Jesus. And immediately he took the child in his arms and said: 'Now I can die in peace, for with my own eyes I have seen the light which you have sent to show truth to the Gentiles and bring glory to the people of Israel.'

Mary and Joseph were amazed at this. Then Simeon turned to Mary and told her: 'This child will decide the fates of many in Israel. But for you . . . you will suffer much sorrow.'

●

St. Matthew 2–1-23

The Wise Men's Visit: and the Rage of Herod

A short while after Jesus's birth, a party of astrologers came from the east travelling towards Jerusalem and asking everyone they met: 'Where is the child who is born to be King of the Jews? We saw his star in the east and are following it. We have come to pay our respects.'

When King Herod heard about this he was very worried, and invited the professors to meet him in private to find out what they knew. He told them: 'Search for this child carefully and, when you have found him, let me know, so that I too can visit him and worship him.'

The wise men left the king and headed for Bethlehem, for the star was now immediately ahead of them and they followed it until it led them to the place where Jesus lay. And, as soon as they saw Jesus with his mother Mary, they went down on their knees to worship him, and then they gave him the gifts they had brought . . . gold, frankincense and myrrh.

When the time came for them to leave, they returned to their own country by a different route for they had been warned in a dream that they should not visit Herod again.

And when they had left, the angel of the Lord appeared to Joseph in a dream and told him, 'Get up, and take Jesus and Mary to Egypt and stay there as long as I tell you to, for Herod will try to kill Jesus.'

Joseph got up straight away and in the middle of the night set off for Egypt with Mary and Jesus.

When Herod realized that the wise men had tricked him, he was furious, and issued instructions for every boy child under the age of two in and around Bethlehem to be killed. And this was done.

Some time later, Herod died and an angel again came to Joseph in a dream and told him that it was safe to return to Israel. Joseph did so, taking Mary and Jesus but, when he learned that Herod's son Archelaus was now ruler of Judea, he went instead to Nazareth in the district of Galilee.

●

St. Luke 2–39-40, 51-52

Here the child grew up, strong, wise and good.

●

Jesus and the Temple Elders

When Jesus was twelve years old, he went with his parents to Jerusalem for the annual Passover celebration. When it was over, Joseph and Mary headed back for home with a large group of travellers and had journeyed for a whole day before they realized that Jesus wasn't with them. They looked for him amongst the company but found he wasn't there, so they turned back towards Jerusalem. On the third day they found him in the Temple surrounded by teachers, asking them questions and answering *their* questions. People watching were amazed at his cleverness, including Mary and Joseph who could hardly believe their eyes.

Mary, still upset by how worried she had been, said, 'My son, why have you done this? We have been looking everywhere for you. Your father and I were desperately worried.'

And Jesus replied, 'Didn't you know that I have work to do for my Father?'

They didn't understand him but Mary later remembered these sayings and often thought about them.

CHAPTER TWO

St. Matthew 3; St. Mark 1; St. Luke 3; St. John 1

John the Baptist meets Jesus

Now, many years later, it happened that John (son of Elisabeth and Zacharias) began preaching in the Judean desert. He wore rough clothes of camel hair with a simple leather thong tied around his waist, and lived on locusts and honey. People flocked to him from miles around, publicly confessed their sins and were baptised in the River Jordan at Bethany. They called him John the Baptist.

John would tell the people, 'It is true that I baptise you with water but that alone is not enough. Make sure that *you* change your way of life and turn over a new leaf. The man who has two shirts must give one to the man who has nothing. The man who has food must share his with the man who is without food.'

He warned the tax-collectors to take only the correct amount of taxes, and the soldiers to be honest and not bully people.

Some people talked about John and thought that he might be the promised Messiah. But he told them, 'Another will come, who is stronger than I, in fact I am not good enough to untie his shoe laces.'

Then Jesus came to be baptised by John.

'Surely it is I who should be baptised by you,' said John. But Jesus insisted that John baptise him and this was done.

And, as Jesus came up out of the water, the sky opened and the Spirit of God came down like a dove and settled upon him and a voice from heaven said, 'This is my beloved son, in whom I am well pleased. Listen to what he has to say.'

St. Matthew 4; St. Mark 1; St. Luke 4; St. John 1

The Temptation in the Desert

Then the Spirit of God sent Jesus out into the desert to be tempted by the Devil. He was alone, and ate nothing for forty days and forty nights.

Then the Devil came to him and said, 'If you are the Son of God take these stones and turn them into bread.'

Jesus refused.

Then the Devil brought Jesus to Jerusalem and took him up to the highest ledge of the Temple there and said, 'If you are the Son of God throw yourself down from here and see if the angels save you.'

Again Jesus refused.

Then the Devil took Jesus to the top of a very high mountain and pointed to all the kingdoms of the world and said, 'See all this. I will give it all to you if you will worship me.'

And Jesus replied, 'We have been taught that we must only worship God.'

And the Devil went away, and the angels came to Jesus and cared for him.

CHAPTER THREE

St. Luke 3–19-20

John Imprisoned

Round about this time Herod the Tetrarch (a descendant of King Herod) who had been criticised by John for many evil acts, retaliated by putting John in prison.

•

St. Matthew 4; St. Mark 1; St. Luke 4

Jesus Begins His Ministry

When Jesus heard the news of John's arrest he went to live in Capernaum, a town on the edge of a lake, and he began to preach. He was about thirty years old.

'Change your hearts,' he told people. 'For the kingdom of heaven has arrived.'

Very quickly Jesus became famous throughout Syria for his teaching that the kingdom of God had arrived. He healed the sick, and people who were ill were brought to him. Wherever he went he was followed by huge crowds and everybody praised him.

•

St. Matthew 11–2-6, St. Luke 7–18-23

John's Question

Reports of what Jesus was doing reached the ears of John the Baptist in prison and he called two of his disciples and gave them a message to take to Jesus.

'Are you the one we have been waiting for, or are we to go on waiting for someone else?'

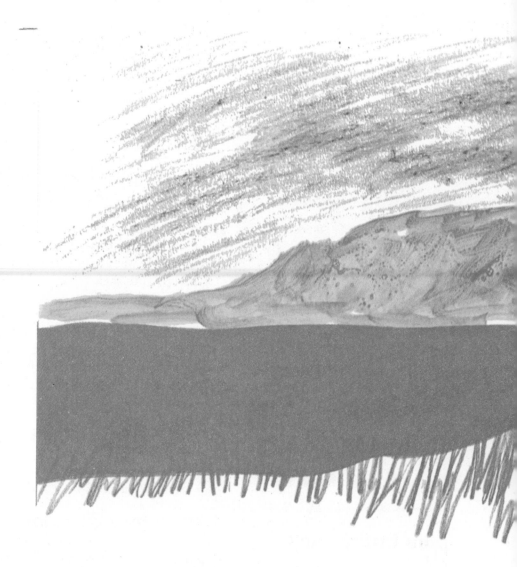

The disciples went to Jesus and put his question to him, and he replied, 'Go back to John and tell him what you have seen and heard. That the blind are made to see, cripples walk, lepers are healed, the deaf are made to hear and dead men are restored to life. The good news is being given to those who need it. And happy is the man who does not lose faith in me.'

•

St. Matthew 4; St. Mark 1; St. Luke 5

Jesus Calls His Disciples

One day Jesus was walking by the lake of Galilee when he saw two fishermen, Simon Peter and Andrew who were brothers, casting their net into the water.

'Come follow me,' he said, 'and I will make you fishers of men.' At once they left their nets and followed him.

A little further on he met two more men, James and John, who were also brothers, mending their nets on a fishing boat, with their father, Zebedee. He called to them and they left their father and their boat and went with him.

•

St. John 1–35-51

Jesus Calls Nathanael

Then Jesus met Philip and said, 'Follow me.' Philip who came from the same town as Simon Peter and Andrew, had a friend called Nathanael (sometimes called Bartholomew) and he told him, 'We have found the one Moses and the prophets wrote about. He is Jesus, son of Joseph. He comes from Nazareth.'

'Can anyone special come from such an insignificant place as Nazareth?' asked Nathanael sceptically.

'Come and meet him for yourself,' said Philip.

When Jesus saw them coming, he said, 'Here is a true Israelite. An honest man.'

'Do you know me then?' asked Nathanael.

'Before Philip came to call you,' said Jesus. 'I saw you under a fig tree.'

Nathanael was astonished. 'Teacher, you really are the Son of God, King of Israel,' he said.

Jesus replied. 'What, just because I said that I saw you under a fig tree? I assure you that's nothing to what you will see. I promise you, you will see heaven wide open and God's angels ascending and descending around the Son of Man.'

He, of course, had no idea where it had come from, but said to Jesus, 'At most parties the host gives people the best wine first and saves the cheaper stuff until they've had plenty to drink. But you have kept the best wine until now.'

St. John 2–1–10

Jesus Changes Water into Wine

Jesus, his mother and his disciples were guests at a wedding at Cana in Galilee. During the festivities Jesus's mother turned to him and said, 'They have run out of wine, it is all used up.'

'Why tell me?' said Jesus. But nevertheless his mother turned to the servants and said 'Do whatever he tells you.'

Nearby were standing six stone jars used to hold water for the Jewish purification rites. They were large jars. Each could hold twenty or thirty gallons.

'Fill them with water,' Jesus instructed and they were filled to the brim. 'Now draw some out and take it to the wine steward.' This they did; the steward tasted the water and it had changed into wine.

Only the servants and the disciples knew what Jesus had done. The servants did not understand, but the disciples knew, and believed in him.

her, and taking her hand helped her to her feet. Immediately the fever left her.

Throughout the evening, the people of the town gathered at the door of the house, bringing to him all their sick friends and relatives, and he healed many.

Early in the morning, before it was light, Jesus left the house and went to a deserted place and prayed. Simon Peter and the others looked for him, and when they found him they told him that everybody was looking for him.

'Then we shall go to other towns, so that I can give my message to other people,' said Jesus. 'That is what I am here for.'

•

St. Matthew 8; St. Mark 1; St. Luke 5

Jesus and the Leper

One day a man came to him who was covered with the sores of leprosy. He knelt before Jesus, imploring, 'Please cure me.'

And Jesus was filled with pity for the man, and touched him, saying, 'Be clean.'

St. Mark 1–21-28, St. Luke 4–31-37

Jesus Heals the Sick

They went to Capernaum. On the Sabbath, Jesus entered the synagogue and started to teach. Everybody was astonished by the knowledgeable way he spoke.

A mad man came near to Jesus, shouting at him. Jesus spoke sharply to the evil spirit inside the man. 'Get out of him.'

The evil spirit gave a loud scream and left the man, and the man was calm and no longer mad.

Of course this astonished the people who were watching even further.

Jesus left the synagogue and went to the house of Simon Peter and Andrew, with James and John. When he arrived there, he learned that Simon Peter's mother-in-law was ill in bed. He went to

At once the man's leprosy vanished, and Jesus told him to go straight away and show himself to the priest at the Temple, but to tell nobody else about it.

But the man went away and talked to a great many people about what had happened to him and consequently Jesus became so famous that he had to stay outside the towns, but still the people managed to find him.

•

St. Matthew 8, St. Luke 7

The Soldier's Servant

One day a Roman soldier approached him. 'Sir, my servant is paralysed and in terrible pain,' he said.

'I will come and heal him,' replied Jesus.

But the soldier said, 'Just give the order, and my servant will recover. It is not important enough for you to travel to my house. Your order will cure him.'

Jesus was astonished at the man's great faith, and he said to the Roman soldier, 'Go home and everything will be as you believe.'

And the servant was healed immediately.

•

St. Matthew 9; St. Mark 2; St. Luke 5

The Paralysed Man

One day when he was at Capernaum a rumour spread that he was in a certain house. Such a huge crowd collected that it was impossible to reach the doorway. A group of four arrived, carrying between them a paralysed man. They realised that they could not get to Jesus through the vast crowd, so they climbed onto the roof, removed some tiles and let down the paralytic on his bed through the hole in the roof.

Jesus, seeing their faith, said to the man on the bed, 'My son, your sins are forgiven.'

Some scribes, overhearing this were offended and thought, 'This is blasphemy. Only God can forgive sins.'

Jesus knew what they were thinking and said to them, 'What do you think means more to a paralysed man? To say "your sins are forgiven" or to say "pick up your bed and walk"? But to prove that I have authority to forgive sins on earth, I say (and he turned to the paralysed man) "Stand up, pick up your bed and walk home."'

Then the man sprang to his feet, took up his bed and walked away, watched by everyone.

•

St. Matthew 9; St. Mark 2, St. Luke 5

Jesus Tells: Why I am Here

In the course of his day-to-day life, Jesus met Matthew who was a tax-collector. 'Follow me,' said Jesus, and Matthew left his desk and followed him. Later they were having dinner at Matthew's house with Jesus's disciples and many other tax-collectors and also some disreputable characters were there. The scribes and Pharisees saw what was happening and they asked the disciples, 'Why does he eat and drink with these awful people?'

But Jesus overheard and he said: 'The healthy don't need a doctor, but the sick do. I didn't come to guide the people who are good already, I came to guide the sinners.'

•

St. Matthew 10; St. Mark 3; St. Luke 6

The Twelve are Chosen

Jesus went up the hill and found a flat place and spent the night praying. When it was morning, he called his closest followers and chose from amongst them twelve men whom he could send out to preach and who would have the power to drive out evil spirits. The men were Simon Peter, James and John, Andrew, Philip, Bartholomew, Matthew, Thomas, James (son of Alphaeus), Thaddaeus, Simon and Judas Iscariot who became a traitor.

CHAPTER FOUR

St. Matthew 5, 6 and 7

The Sermon on the Mount

They sat down together, and Jesus spoke to them.

'Those who are humble shall be given heaven.

Those who are sad shall be given courage and comfort.

Those who are patient shall be given the earth.

Those who look for goodness will be given it.

Those who show mercy to others will receive mercy.

Those who are honest in their hearts will see God.

Those who make peace shall be known as the sons of God. And those who have been persecuted for their goodness shall be given heaven.

If you are wronged by others because you support me, be glad, for your reward in heaven will be truly wonderful.

Men do not light a lamp then hide it under a bucket. They put the lamp where everyone can see it, and where it can give light for others to see by. Let your light shine like that. Let men see the good things you do and praise your Father in heaven.

You have heard the saying "An eye for an eye, a tooth for a tooth." Well I say if a man hits your right cheek, turn your left cheek as well. You have heard it said "Love your neighbour and hate your enemy." Well I say love your enemies as well, for God makes the sun rise for evil men as well as good, and sends his rain upon honest men as well as dishonest.

Do not show off when you are doing a good deed. If you give money to charity do so in secret. Your Father knows all secrets and will reward you.

When you pray do so in the privacy of your own room, with the door closed. And pray like this:

'Our Father who art in heaven,
hallowed be your name
your kingdom come,
your will be done
on earth as it is in heaven.
Give us this day,
our daily bread
and forgive us our debts,
as we forgive our debtors.
And lead us not into temptation
but deliver us from evil.

Don't hoard treasures on earth where they can go rusty and moth-eaten. Keep your treasure safe in heaven. Don't worry about living, or what you are going to eat or drink or wear. Your heavenly Father knows that you need food and drink and clothes and he will provide them. The one who asks will always have it given to him, in the same way as the one who is looking will always find what he is looking for.

Behave towards others as you would like them to behave towards yourself.

Be on your guard against dishonest preachers who come dressed as sheep but are really wolves in disguise.

And having heard my words, pay attention to them. For to ignore them would be like the man who built his house on sand, and when the rain, floods and wind came the house was battered down because he had built it with no foundations'.

CHAPTER FIVE

St. Matthew 9; St. Mark 2; St. Luke 5

Jesus Explains

One day John's disciples asked Jesus, 'We and the Pharisees fast, but your disciples do nothing of the sort. Why should this be?'

And Jesus replied, 'Would guests at a wedding fast whilst the bridegroom was there? The day will come when the bridegroom is taken away from them and they will fast then.'

Jesus Calms the Storm

Jesus and his disciples were aboard a boat crossing the lake, when a fierce storm blew up, rocking the boat and sending the waves pounding over its decks. Jesus was asleep, and his disciples woke him crying 'Lord, save us, for we are drowning.'

Jesus stood up. 'Be quiet,' he said to the wind and the waves, and the wind dropped and the water was calm.

Then he turned to his disciples, 'What has happened to your faith,' he said. 'Why are you so frightened?'

And they were astonished and asked themselves 'What kind of a man is this who can tell the wind and the waves what to do and they obey him?'

●

St. Matthew 8–28-34

The Gadarene Maniac

When they arrived at the far side of the Lake in the region of the Gadarene a mad man appeared from among the tombs. He was an outcast, who screamed day and night and stuck jagged stones into himself. As soon as he saw Jesus he ran to him and knelt, shouting, 'What have you got to do with me Jesus, son of the most High God. For God's sake, don't torture me.'

'What is your name?' asked Jesus.

'Legion,' the mad man replied, 'meaning there are many inside me.'

Nearby a herd of pigs was grazing on the hillside, and Jesus instructed the evil spirits to leave the man and go into the pigs. And immediately the herd of pigs went mad and stampeded over the cliff top into the water below and were drowned.

And the man who had been mad was now sane and calm.

And when the people in the town saw what had happened they were afraid and begged Jesus to go away.

●

St. Matthew 14–3-13, St. Mark 6–17-29

The Death of John the Baptist

John the Baptist was still chained in prison for having dared to criticize Herod. In particular he had publicly condemned Herod for marrying his own brother's wife, Herodias. Herodias wanted John the Baptist killed for this, but Herod was afraid to go too far, knowing that John was a good and holy man.

Then it was Herod's birthday and he gave a great party for all the important people in his court, and the officers in his army, and the most influential people in Galilee. During the celebrations Salome, the daughter of Herodias came into the banquet room and danced for the guests, who were so delighted with her performance that Herod promised her: 'Ask for whatever you like and I shall give it to you . . . half my kingdom if you want it.'

Salome went outside and asked her mother what should she say. And her mother replied, 'Ask for the head of John the Baptist.'

So the girl went back into the banquet room and said to Herod, 'I want you to give me John the Baptist's head at once, on a dish.'

The king was very upset by this turn of events, but having made such a sweeping promise so publicly, he felt he could not break his word. Turning to one of his bodyguards he instructed him to bring John's head. The soldier went straight away to the prison, beheaded the prisoner John and returned with his head on a dish which he gave to Salome. And she gave it to her mother.

Later John's disciples heard about this and took his body and laid it in a tomb. Then they went to Jesus to tell him what had happened and, when he had listened to their news, he went away by boat to a quiet place where he was alone.

St. Matthew 10; St. Mark 6; St. Luke 9

Jesus Instructs the Twelve

Then Jesus called the twelve disciples together and sent them off in pairs with these instructions: 'Concentrate on the lost sheep of the house of Israel. Tell them that the kingdom of heaven has arrived. Heal the sick, restore the dead to life. Take no money with you, carry no food for the journey, nor even a change of clothes.

The Feeding of the Five Thousand

When the disciples returned from their travels, they wanted to tell Jesus of their experiences so they all went with him to a town called Bethsaida, to talk privately. But the people from the neighbouring towns and villages found out where he was and clamoured to follow him.

Jesus took pity on them because he thought they were like sheep without a shepherd, so throughout the day, he talked to them and healed them until it

'When you enter a house, give it your blessing. But if people will not welcome you, nor even listen to you, then don't waste your time on them.'

So they went on their way, preaching and healing.

●

St. Matthew 14; St. Mark 6; St. Luke 9

Herod's Fears

Some people believed that Jesus was Elijah, and others believed that Jesus was one of the old prophets restored to life again. News of what Jesus was doing reached the ears of Herod who found the stories alarming.'It must be John, risen from the dead,' he thought. And he was anxious to see Jesus for himself.

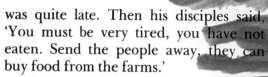

was quite late. Then his disciples said, 'You must be very tired, you have not eaten. Send the people away, they can buy food from the farms.'

Jesus replied, 'There's no need for that. You feed them.'

The disciples were dismayed for there were five thousand people in the crowd. 'How are we to do that?' they asked Jesus.

'Go and see how much food you have,' said Jesus, and they did, and they told him that they had found a boy who had five loaves of bread and two fishes.

Then Jesus told them to make all the people sit down, in groups, and when this had been done, he took the five loaves and the two fishes, raised his eyes to heaven and blessed the food. Then he broke the bread and the fishes, and handed the pieces to the disciples to share among the people.

Everyone ate as much as he or she wanted and when they had all finished the disciples collected the leftover scraps and filled twelve baskets full.

•

St. Matthew 14; St. Mark 6; St. Luke 9;
St. John 6

Jesus Walks on Water

While Jesus was sending the crowds home, he told the disciples to go on ahead to the other side of the lake. When he was ready to join them he could see that they were exhausted with rowing against the wind, and he went out to join them, walking on the water. When they saw this ghostly figure walking on the lake they were terrified, but he told them 'Don't be afraid, it is I, Jesus.'

'Lord, if it is really you, make me come to you over the waters too,' said Simon Peter.

'Come on then,' Jesus replied. And Simon Peter stepped down from the boat and started to walk towards Jesus but, when he realized what he was doing and saw the fierce waves, he lost his nerve and began to sink, crying for help and saying, 'Lord, save me.'

And Jesus stretched out his hand and saved him. 'Why did you panic,' he asked. 'What happened to your faith?'

They both climbed into the boat then the wind dropped and the disciples knelt before Jesus and said, 'You are indeed the Son of God.'

•

The Man with the Withered Hand

Jesus went into the synagogue one Sabbath day to teach, and there was a man there with a withered hand. The scribes and the Pharisees were watching Jesus to see if he would break their Sabbath laws by curing the man. They were hoping for some evidence to use against him in this respect. But Jesus knew exactly what was going on in their minds, and he called the man to stand up and walk into the middle of the synagogue. Then he pointed to the man and he said, to the scribes and Pharisees, 'Is it against the law on the Sabbath day to do good, or bad? To save life or to kill?' Nobody answered him, and he said 'If you had a sheep which fell into a ditch on the Sabbath day, surely you would pull it out. Isn't a man's life more valuable than a sheep's?'

Obstinately they did not answer and Jesus looked angrily at them all. Then he said to the man 'Stretch out your hand.'

The man put out his withered hand, and it was healed.

Then the Pharisees left the synagogue and at once joined with Herod's supporters to plot a way of destroying Jesus.

•

The Cure of the Deaf Mute

One day Jesus was preaching to a crowd when some people pushed a way through bringing a man who was deaf and dumb, asking Jesus to heal the man. He took the man away from the crowd to where it was quiet, put his fingers into the man's ears, and touched the man's tongue with spittle. Then, looking up to heaven he said, 'Be opened.'

And at once the man's ears were 'opened' and he could hear, and at the same time he could speak. Jesus told the crowd not to discuss what had happened, but they were so full of admiration and wonder that they went away and told everybody.

•

The Blind Man of Bethsaida

Arriving at the town of Bethsaida, Jesus was met by some people who had with them a blind man whom they begged him to heal. Jesus took the blind man by the hand and led him away from the houses. Then he put spittle on the blind man's eyes and, touching him, asked 'Can you see anything?'

The man replied 'I can see people who look like trees, walking about.' Then Jesus laid his hands on the man's eyes a second time, whereupon the man could see everything clearly and distinctly, and he was cured.

•

Jairus's Daughter: and the Woman in the Crowd

Jesus was preaching beside the lake, surrounded by many people, when a man called Jairus, an official at the synagogue, pushed his way through to Jesus and fell on his knees imploring 'My little girl is desperately ill. Please come at once.'

Jesus tried to follow Jairus to the house where the child lay, but the crowd was thick and he had to battle his way through. Among the people who had come to see him that day was a woman who had suffered from a bleeding disease for twelve years. She had suffered all sorts of painful treatments, and had spent all her money on doctors' bills, and was getting steadily worse. She had heard about Jesus and had come to see him and now she squeezed her way through the crowd and stretched out her hand for she felt that if she could only touch some part of him she would get well.

And as her fingers touched his cloak, the bleeding inside her ceased, and she knew that she was cured. But Jesus stopped.

'Who touched me?' he asked.

His disciples said, 'People are touching you all the time . . . look at the crowd pushing.'

But Jesus said 'Somebody touched me, I felt power going from me.' And as he continued to look around the woman came forward, frightened and trembling, and she fell at his feet and told him the truth.

And Jesus told her, 'My daughter, your faith has cured you.'

Whilst he was still talking to her, some people arrived from Jairus's house to say that Jairus's daughter had died.

'It's too late to do anything to help her,' they said. 'Don't waste Jesus's time.'

But Jesus overheard this and he said to Jairus, 'Have faith,' then hurried to the house where there was a great deal of

weeping and wailing going on.

'Be quiet and go outside,' he told them. 'The child is not dead, she is asleep.' Some of the onlookers laughed scornfully at this, but nevertheless they went outside and Jesus allowed only the parents of the child, and Simon Peter, James and James' brother, John, to remain.

Then he went to the bed where the child lay, and taking her hand he said, 'Little girl, do as I say, and get up.'

And she got up at once and began to walk about. Her parents were amazed and overjoyed, and Jesus told them to give her something to eat.

•

St. Luke 7–11-17

The Widow of Nain

Jesus went to a town called Nain, accompanied by his disciples and followed by a great crowd of people. And, as he approached the town gates, he passed a funeral procession, and the dead man was the only son of a widow, who was deeply distressed. Jesus felt sorry for her.

'Don't cry,' he said. Then he went to the stand on which the corpse was being carried. The bearers stood still, and Jesus said, 'Young man I tell you to get up.'

And the dead man sat up and started talking. Jesus had given the widow back her son.

The people were overawed and

praised God. 'He has sent a great leader to us,' they said and as the stories about Jesus were told throughout the land, many people had the same opinion.

•

St. Luke 13–10-17

The Bent Woman

One Sabbath day when he was teaching in a synagogue, he saw a woman who was bent double and couldn't stand upright. She had suffered this deformity for eighteen years. Jesus called her to him and said, 'Woman, you are cured.' He put his hands on her, and she at once stood up straight, and praised God.

But the synagogue official, who had seen what happened, was indignant and spoke to all the people saying, 'God gave us six days for work. If you want to be healed come on one of these work days and not on the Sabbath.'

Then Jesus answered him. 'Hypocrites,' he said. 'Is there one person here who does not untie his ox on the Sabbath so that the animal can drink water? And this woman has been tied for eighteen years, isn't it right to untie her bonds on the Sabbath?'

His enemies found all this very confusing and embarrassing, but the people were overjoyed at the marvellous things he did.

•

The Epileptic

One day when Jesus's disciples were preaching to the crowd, Jesus approached and saw that an argument was going on. As soon as they saw him, the people surged towards him.

'Why are you arguing?' he asked.

A man from the crowd answered, 'Master I have an only son. There is an evil spirit inside him, it has made him dumb and sometimes it makes him fall to the ground, foam at the mouth and grind his teeth. His body goes rigid. I brought him here, and asked your disciples to cast out the evil spirit but they cannot.'

'You faithless lot,' said Jesus. 'How much longer must I put up with you?'

They brought the boy forward and, as soon as he came before Jesus, he fell to the ground, writhing, foaming at the mouth.

'How long has he had this condition?' Jesus asked the father, who replied 'Since childhood. Sometimes the evil spirit has thrown the boy into fire or water in an effort to destroy him. Please take pity on us and help.'

'Everything is possible if you have faith,' said Jesus.

'I do have faith,' cried the father of the boy.

Then Jesus rebuked the spirit. 'Deaf and dumb spirit,' he commanded, 'come out at once and never enter this boy again.'

At once the boy went into convulsions, shouting, then fell to the ground and lay so corpselike that some people thought he was dead. Jesus took him by the hand, helped him to his feet and he was cured.

The disciples, when they were alone with him, asked Jesus, 'Why couldn't we cure the boy?'

And he answered, 'Because you don't have enough faith. I tell you that if your faith was the size of a mustard seed you could say to a mountain "Move from here to there" and it would move. With faith nothing would be impossible for you.

Were your faith the size of a mustard seed you could say to this mulberry tree "Be uprooted and planted in the sea" and it would obey you.'

•

The Ten Lepers

One day as Jesus was approaching a village he heard voices calling him and saw, standing a distance away, ten lepers.

'Jesus, Master take pity on us,' they shouted.

Jesus replied, 'Go and show yourselves to the priest,' and as they turned away to do as he had told them, their sores disappeared and they were cured.

One of them, a Samaritan, realising that he was well, turned back and threw himself at the feet of Jesus and thanked him.

'Where are the others?' said Jesus. 'Weren't all ten of you cured? Where are the other nine? It seems that the only one who has bothered to thank God is this foreigner.'

Then he told the man, 'Go on your way . . . your faith has saved you.'

•

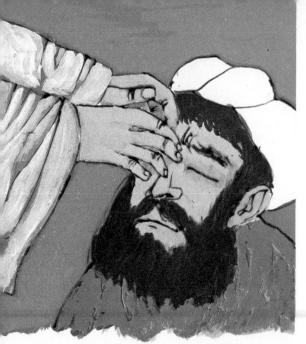

St. John 9–1-34

The Blind Beggar

One day Jesus saw a blind beggar, the man had been born blind and many people said that his blindness was God's way of punishing the parents' sins. But Jesus said, 'His parents did not sin, this man's blindness is an opportunity for God's work to be displayed.'

And with these words he spat on the ground, mixed some spittle and earth into a paste and put this on the blind man's eyes. Then he told him to go and wash in a nearby pool. The blind man did so and immediately could see.

Then neighbours who had known him said, 'Surely this isn't the same man who used to sit and beg?' Some said it was the same man, others said it was a man who looked like him.

But the man, hearing the speculations, said, 'I am that man.'

So they asked him, 'Then how is it you are no longer blind?' And he told them what Jesus had done.

So they took the man to the Pharisees, and he repeated his story about Jesus. The Pharisees were divided amongst themselves. Those who knew that Jesus had cured the man on the Sabbath were very angry. Others refused to believe that the man had ever been blind in the first place so they sent for his parents to check his story.

His parents were afraid of the synagogue leaders who had already threatened to expel anybody who said that Jesus was Christ. So, when the Pharisees asked them how the blindness was cured, they replied, 'This is our son. He was born blind. Now he can see. As to how he was cured, you'd better ask him. He's old enough to speak for himself.'

So they sent for the man again, and made him repeat his story, going over all the details. And they said to him, 'We know that God spoke to Moses, but as for this man Jesus, we don't know where he comes from.'

And the man replied, 'You astonish me. Since the beginning of the world it has been unheard of for a blind man to see. If this man Jesus is not from God, how could he do this?'

At this the Pharisees were furious and drove the man away.

●

St. John 5–1-18

Miracle at Bethesda

In Jerusalem there was a sheep pool surrounded by five covered colonnades and the place was called Bethesda. Under these colonnades gathered a great many sick people, blind, lame, paralysed, waiting for the water to move for there

carry it,' he replied.

'Who is the man who told you this?' they asked, but he had no idea who it was, for Jesus had slipped away into the dense crowd the moment the man was well.

But later that day Jesus met him again, in the Temple. 'Now that you are a fit man,' he said, 'be careful not to sin again for something worse might happen to you.'

Then the man went to the Jews who had questioned him and told them that the one who had cured him was Jesus.

The Jews were opposed to Jesus because he did these things on the Sabbath. Jesus's reply to this attitude was to say, 'My Father goes on working, and so do I.'

And this made the Jews even more determined to kill him because not only did he break their Sabbath laws but he referred to God as his own Father and so put himself on equal terms with God.

was a tradition that from time to time an angel would come down and move the waters of the pool, and that the first person to enter the waters after they had been disturbed in this manner would be cured.

Jesus was visiting Jerusalem for one of the religious festivals, and noticed a man lying at Bethesda and the man had been waiting there for thirty-eight years.

Knowing this, Jesus asked him, 'Do you want to get well again?'

'Sir,' said the sick man, 'I have nobody to lift me into the pool when the water is stirred up. By the time I get to the pool somebody else has already managed to get into the water before me.'

'Get up,' said Jesus. 'Pick up your sleeping mat, and walk.' At once the man recovered, picked up his sleeping mat and walked away.

It was the Sabbath day, and certain Jews said to the man, 'You know you shouldn't be carrying your sleeping mat on the Sabbath.'

'The man who cured me told me to

CHAPTER SIX

St. Matthew 13; St. Mark 4; St. Luke 8

Jesus Teaches

Often when Jesus taught the people, he told them 'parables' or picture stories to help them understand his preachings.

A large crowd gathered around Jesus, so large in fact that he climbed into a boat in order to be able to speak to them all, and they sat or stood on the beach listening to him.

•

St. Matthew 13; St. Mark 4; St. Luke 8

The Parable of the Seeds

'Imagine,' said Jesus, 'a farmer going out to sow some seeds. As he worked some seeds fell on the edge of the path where they were quickly eaten up by the birds. Some seeds fell on the stones and rocks where there was a little soil. They sprang up but as soon as the sun shone they withered and, having weak roots, died. Others fell among thorns and weeds and were choked. Others fell on rich soil and these grew strong and healthy and produced a rich crop.'

•

St. Matthew 13; St. Mark 4; St. Luke 8

The Parable of the Seeds Explained

Then he explained the meaning of this story to his disciples. For the seed, he said, was the word of God. Those on the edge of the path are people who hear the word but before it takes root in their heart the Devil comes and carries it off. The man who hears it on the rocky ground is the one who welcomes it, but his enthusiasm doesn't last and the first time he is put to the test the word withers and dies because it has no roots in him. The one who receives it in the thorns and weeds, is the one who hears the word but

is more concerned with the material things of life, and the word is choked by the lure of riches. And the one who receives the word in rich soil is the one who hears and truly understands and shares his harvest with others.

•

St. Luke 10—25-37

The Good Samaritan

On one occasion when Jesus was preaching to a large crowd, a young lawyer who thought he could trick Jesus, stood up and asked 'What must I do to be sure of eternal life?'

'What does the Law tell you, and what have you learned from your reading?' asked Jesus.

The young man replied, 'It is written that I must love God with all my heart, with all my soul and with all my strength. And I must love my neighbour as much as I love myself.'

'That's right,' said Jesus. 'Well if you follow those rules, you can be sure of eternal life.'

But the man pressed the point further. 'Who is my neighbour?' he asked.

Then Jesus told him a story.

A man was travelling from Jerusalem to Jericho, along a lonely road, when he was attacked by a gang of robbers who beat him almost to death and escaped with all his money.

A priest happened to be travelling along the same road, and when he saw the man's beaten body lying by the road-side, he crossed to the other side of the road and passed by without stopping. Some time afterwards one of the Temple assistants also came along the road, and seeing the injured man he too crossed over and passed on the other side.

Then a third man came along, a Samaritan. When he saw the man lying there, he felt very sorry for him. Kneeling down, he washed his wounds with the oil and wine which he was carrying and bandaged them. Then he lifted the man onto his own horse and took him to the nearest inn. He gave the innkeeper some money and instructed him, 'Look after this man. On my return journey I will call in and if you have had any additional expense I will make it good.'

I have no food for him. Please lend me some bread." And the man inside replies, "Go away, we're all in bed and the door is bolted."

'Well if that man who wants to borrow some bread persists, knocking at the door and refusing to go away without it, his friend will eventually have to give in, not out of friendship but simply to get rid of the man outside. And he will get up and give the man what he wants.

'And this is what you should do. You should ask, and it will be given to you. Knock and the door will be opened. The one who searches always finds. No father would give his child a stone when it asks for bread, or hand him a snake when he asked for fish. So if earthly fathers have that much feeling for their children, imagine how much more benevolent God is, and how eager to give the Holy Spirit to those who ask for it.'

●

Then Jesus turned to the young lawyer and said, 'Which of the three men proved to be a neighbour to the man who had been attacked?'

'Why, the one who took pity on him,' said the lawyer.

'Then go and do the same,' replied Jesus.

●

St. Luke 11–5-13

Jesus says: Don't be Afraid to Ask

Another time Jesus said, 'Imagine a man goes to his friend in the middle of the night, knocking at the door and asking "A guest has just arrived at my house and

Then he said, 'The kingdom of heaven is like treasure hidden in a field. A man discovers the buried treasure, hides it again then goes away and sells everything he owns so that he can buy the field.

'Again, the kingdom of heaven is like the merchant who is looking for fine pearls. When he finds what he is looking for, a pearl of great value, he sells everything he owns in order to buy it.'

●

St. Matthew 13; St. Mark 4; St. Luke 13

Pictures of Heaven

Jesus was describing to the crowd what was meant by the kingdom of heaven.

'It is like a mustard seed,' he said, 'which a man took and planted in a field. The mustard seed is the smallest of all seeds, but when it grows it is the biggest of all the shrubs and sends out strong branches and the birds come and make their nests in it.'

St. Matthew 13—24-30

Parable of the Weeds

'You could say that the kingdom of heaven is like the man who sowed good seed in his field. Then, when everybody was asleep, his enemy crept into the field and sowed weeds among the wheat, then went away.

'The new wheat sprouted but so did the weeds and the man's servants said, "That must have been poor quality seed." But the man guessed what had happened. "Some enemy has done this" he told them.

"hall we go and weed it out?" said the servants. But that wasn't a practical idea. "You might pull up the wheat with the weeds," said the man.

"No, let them both grow until it is time for the harvest. Then the reapers can collect the weeds, tie them in bundles and burn them. And the wheat will be gathered and stored in my barn."'

•

St. Matthew 13–36–43

Parable of the Weeds Explained

Turning to his disciples Jesus explained, 'The man who sowed the good seeds is the Son of Man, the field is the world and the good seed is all the subjects of his kingdom. The man who crept into the field is the Devil and the weeds he sowed are the evil people. The harvest is the end of the world, and the reapers are the angels.

'Just as weeds are gathered up and burned, so those who defy God will be destroyed in a blazing fire. It will be too late for tears of regret.

'And the good will remain to shine out like the sun.'

•

St. Matthew 13–47-50

Heaven – and a Fishing Net

'Similarly the kingdom of heaven is like a net thrown into the sea. When it is full, the fishermen pull it in and, once it is ashore, they proceed to sort out their catch. They put the good fish into a basket and throw away those which aren't any good.

'And this is how it will be at the end of time, when the angels will separate the good from the bad, and throw the bad into the fire.'

•

St. Matthew 19; St. Mark 10; St. Luke 18

The Rich Man and the Kingdom of Heaven

A rich young man came to Jesus and asked him, 'What good deed must I do to inherit eternal life?'

Jesus replied, 'You must not kill, you must not commit adultery, you must not steal, you must not lie, you must obey your mother and father and you must love your neighbour as much as you love yourself.'

The young man said, 'I have followed all these rules all my life. What else is there?'

And Jesus said, 'If you want to be perfect , go and sell all your possessions and give the money to the poor, then you will have treasure in heaven. Come, follow me.'

But the young man's face showed how disappointed he was to hear these words, and he went away.

And Jesus told his disciples, 'It will be very hard for a rich man to enter the kingdom of heaven. In fact it would be easier for a camel to pass through the eye of a needle than for a rich man to enter the kingdom of heaven.'

•

Jesus and the Woman's Tears

Jesus accepted an invitation to eat at the house of Simon the Pharisee. After he had taken his place at the table, a woman came in, who had a bad reputation in the town. She had heard that Jesus would be spending the evening there, and brought with her an alabaster jar of ointment. Then she knelt at his feet. As she waited, she wept, and her tears fell onto Jesus's feet. And she wiped them away with her hair. And when she had dried his feet she gently rubbed the costly ointment onto them.

His host, Simon, seeing this, thought, 'If this man had divine powers he would know that this is a bad woman whom he allows to touch him.'

Jesus who knew Simon's thoughts, said, 'Simon, I've something to say to you.'

'Tell me, Master,' said Simon.

And Jesus said, 'There was a man who was owed money by two others. One of them owed him five hundred pieces of silver and the other owed him fifty pieces of silver. Both were unable to pay him the money they owed him, so he excused them both. Which one do you suppose loved him most for this kindness?'

'Why the one who had owed him the greater amount of money, I suppose,' said Simon.

'You are right,' said Jesus. He turned to the woman. 'Simon,' he said, 'you see this woman don't you? I came into your house and you did not offer to wash my feet, but she has washed my feet with her tears and dried them with her hair. You did not kiss me, but she has been showering my feet with kisses ever since I arrived. You didn't give me oil for my head, but she put ointment on my feet.

'And that is how I know that her sins have been forgiven for that is why she has such love and gratitude to offer.'

Then he said to the woman, 'Your sins have been forgiven.'

Then the guests at the table said to each other, 'Who is he to forgive sins?'

But Jesus said to the woman, 'It is your faith that has saved you. Go in peace.'

St. Luke 8–1-3

Jesus Journeys

Jesus visited every town and village preaching and telling people the good news about God's kingdom. He travelled with his twelve disciples, and certain women whom he had healed, such as Mary Magdalene, Joanna (the wife of Herod's agent, Chuza), Susanna and several others who had money to help support him.

•

St. Matthew 18–12-14, St. Luke 15–1-7

Parable of the Lost Sheep

Jesus knew that the scribes and Pharisees complained that he spoke to tax-collectors and sinners, so to explain why he did this he told them the following parables.

'What man with a hundred sheep, having lost one of them would not leave the other ninety-nine and go searching for the missing one. And having found it put it joyfully on his shoulders and carry it home and call all his friends and neighbours for a celebration and say "Isn't it marvellous, I've found my sheep that was lost." In the same way there is more rejoicing in heaven over one sinner who repents than over ninety-nine good men who have no need of repentance.'

Parable of the Lost Coin

'Take another example . . . what woman with ten coins would not, if she lost one of them, light a lamp and sweep the house right through, and search thoroughly until she had found it. Then call her friends and neighbours and say, "Celebrate with me, I've found the money I lost." In the same way there is rejoicing among God's angels over one repentant sinner.'

Parable of the Lost Son

Jesus also told the story of the two sons, one a spendthrift, the other dutiful. The younger son, who was the extravagant one, said to his father, 'Father, let me have my share of the money which would eventually be left to me.' So the father divided his property between the two sons and the younger one took his share and left for a foreign country where he promptly squandered it all on his own pleasures.

When it was all used up he was forced to look for work and got a job feeding pigs. He was so hungry he would willingly have eaten the pig's food, except that he wasn't allowed to. He was on the point of starvation and nobody would lift a finger to help him.

He remembered what it was like at his father's farm.

'My father's servants are better off than I am,' he thought.

'They have more food than they can possibly eat. I will leave this place, and go home, and say to my father, "Father, I don't deserve to be called your son, but may I stay with you as one of your paid servants?"'

So he went back to his father. When he was still some distance away his father saw him and was filled with pity. He ran to him, put his arms around him and kissed him.

'Father, I have sinned against heaven and against you,' said the son. 'I no longer deserve to be called your son.'

But the father called to his servants, 'Hurry, fetch the best clothes and put them on him. Put a ring on his finger and shoes on his feet. And get that calf we've been fattening up, and kill it and we'll have a feast and celebrate. For this is my son. I thought he was dead, but he's alive. He was lost, but I have found him.'

Soon the party was in full swing and the elder son, on his way back from working in the fields, heard all the singing and dancing and seeing one of the servants asked him what was going on.

'Your brother has returned,' said the servant. 'And your father has killed the calf we'd fattened, because his son is home safe and sound.'

The elder brother was very angry when he heard this and hung about outside the house refusing to go in. When his father came outside to persuade him in the elder son burst out angrily 'All these years I've worked hard for you and never once disobeyed your orders, and all that time you never offered as much as a kid for me to celebrate with my

friends. Yet your other son squanders all the money you gave him and then comes back and you kill a calf for him.'

The father replied, 'My son, you have been with me always, and everything I have is yours. But how can we not show our joy now that your brother has returned? I thought he was dead, but here he is, alive. He was lost, and I have found him again.'

●

St. Luke 16–19-31

The Rich Man and the Pauper

Jesus told another parable. 'There was a rich man who dressed in purple and fine linen and lived a life of luxury, feasting magnificently every day. And there was a poor dying man called Lazarus who was put down at the rich man's gate, incapable of moving any further even when the dogs came and licked his sores. He longed to be allowed to eat the scraps that fell from the rich man's table.

'Then both men died. The poor man was carried away by angels to the protection of Abraham. The rich man was buried, and his spirit in the lower world looked up and saw Abraham a long way away, with Lazarus beside him. He cried out "Abraham, pity me. Send Lazarus to dip his finger in cold water and put it on the tip of my tongue, for I am in agony in the flames."

'Abraham replied "My son, when you were alive you enjoyed all the good things, and Lazarus lived a miserable existence. Now he is being comforted and it is your turn to suffer.

"What's more, there is such a great gulf between us that nobody from our side can cross into yours, and nobody from your side can cross into ours."

"In that case," said the rich man's spirit, "I beg you to send Lazarus to my father's house, for I have five brothers, and he could warn them so that they won't have to come to this place of torture."

"They have Moses and the Prophets," said Abraham, "they can listen to them."

"Oh, no, father Abraham," said the rich man, "but if only someone were to return to them from the dead, then they would have to listen."

"If they will not listen to Moses or the Prophets," said Abraham, "Then even someone rising from the dead will not convince them."'

•

St. Matthew 18–21-35

The Parable of the Unforgiving Debtor

Simon Peter asked Jesus, 'Lord, how often must I forgive my brother if he behaves badly towards me – as often as seven times?'

Jesus answered, 'Not seven times, but seventy-seven. If he does something wrong reprove him and if he is sorry forgive him. And if he wrongs you seven times a day and seven times says, "I'm sorry" you must forgive him.'

Then Jesus told the parable of the unforgiving debtor. 'A king,' he said 'decided to square up his accounts with his servants, and began calling in all the people who owed him money.

'A man was brought to him who owed

him over a million pounds, but had no means of repaying the debt. Hearing this, the king declared that the man, his wife, and children must be sold into slavery, and all his possessions confiscated and the money used to pay off some of the debt.

'The man threw himself at the king's feet, pleading to be given another chance and time to earn some money towards repayment. The king felt so sorry for him that he cancelled the debt and the man went free.

'He hadn't gone far when he met a fellow servant who in turn owed him a few shillings. He grabbed him by the neck and began to shake him, "Pay me what you owe me," he demanded. The servant fell at his feet, imploring, "Please give me time and I will pay you," but the other refused, and had the debtor thrown into prison.

'When his fellow servants found out about this they were very upset, and went to the king and told him the whole story. The king sent for the servant. "You wicked man," he said, "I cancelled the debt you owed to me. Surely you were therefore obliged to show the same pity to your fellow servant."

'And, angrily, he handed him over to the prison authorities until he could repay the debt.

'The kingdom of heaven can be compared to that king. And that is how my heavenly Father shall deal with you unless you can sincerely forgive each other.'

St. Matthew 19; St. Mark 10; St Luke 18

Jesus and the Little Children

People even brought babies and small children to Jesus so that he could touch them. The disciples frowned on this and tried to turn the people away, but when Jesus saw what they were doing he was indignant and said to them, 'Don't turn the children away. The kingdom of heaven belongs to little children like these. I tell you solemnly that the people who do not welcome the kingdom of God like a little child will never enter it.'

And he put his hands on the children and blessed them.

Mary and Martha

Jesus came to a village and was welcomed into the home of two women, sisters called Mary and Martha. Martha was immediately very busy preparing food for their guest, whilst Mary sat herself down at Jesus's feet and hung on his every word.

Martha resented this and said to Jesus, 'Can't you see that Mary is leaving me to do all the work. Can't you tell her to help me?'

And Jesus replied, 'Martha, my dear, you have chosen to go to a lot of fuss and bother preparing so many things to eat, yet few dishes are needed . . . in fact one simple thing would do. Mary, on the other hand, has made her choice – in fact she has chosen the best part and you must not interfere with her.'

•

St. John 4–1-42

The Woman at the Well

Jesus was passing through a Samaritan town called Sychar, and, feeling tired, sat down by Jacob's well to rest. It was midday, and very hot; he was alone because his disciples had gone into the town to buy food. A Samaritan woman came to the well to draw water and Jesus said to her, 'Would you give me a drink of water, please.'

Jews did not associate with Samaritans, so the woman, not surprisingly, replied, 'What, you a Jew and you ask me, a Samaritan, for a drink?'

'If you knew what God can give,' replied Jesus, 'and if you knew who it is who is asking for a drink of water, I think you would be asking him for living water.'

The woman said, 'This well is deep and you have nothing to draw water with. Where can you get this living water? And are you a greater man than our ancestor Jacob who gave us this well?'

Jesus said to her, 'Whoever drinks this water will be thirsty again. But whoever drinks the water I give will never be thirsty again. The water I give shall become a spring inside him, welling up into eternal life.'

The woman, still not understanding, said, 'Sir, please give me this special water so that I may stop being thirsty then I won't have to come to this well to draw water any more.'

'Go and fetch your husband,' said Jesus, and the woman replied, 'I haven't got a husband.'

You're right,' said Jesus. 'For although you have had five husbands the one you have now is not your husband at all.'

'Sir,' said the woman, astonished, 'I can see that you are a prophet. Our ancestors worshipped on this hillside . . . but you Jews say that Jerusalem is the place to worship . . .'

Jesus interrupted her. 'Believe me,' he said, 'the time will come when worshipping will not be a question of on this hillside or in Jersualem. You are worshipping with your eyes closed . . . the Jews have their eyes open for the salvation of mankind will come from our race.'

'Oh, yes, I understand that the Messiah is coming,' said the woman. 'And when he comes he will explain everything to us.'

'I who am speaking to you,' said Jesus, 'I am the one.'

Just then, Jesus's disciples returned, somewhat surprised to find him deep in conversation with the woman, and she in turn hurried away back to the town (in such haste that she forgot her water pot) to tell everybody, 'Come quickly to see this man who has told me things about myself and my past life. Can this be the Christ?'

Soon a crowd of people began streaming out of the town towards Jesus, many of them already believing in Jesus because the woman had said to them 'He told me everything I've ever done.' They begged him to stay and talk to them and he stayed for two days, and when he left they told the woman, 'We don't believe now just because of what you said, but because we have now heard him with our own ears and we know that this must be the man who will save the world.'

●

St. Matthew 16; St. Mark 8; St. Luke 9

Jesus Warns His Disciples of What Lies Ahead

One day when Jesus was praying with his disciples, he asked them, 'Who do people say I am?'

They answered him that some people said he was John the Baptist, others Elijah, others Jeremiah or one of the prophets.

'But you,'he said, 'who do you say I am?'

And Simon Peter replied, 'You are Christ the Son of God.'

'You are a lucky man,' said Jesus, 'for my Father in heaven has revealed this to you. Now I tell you that you are Peter (which means rock) and on this rock I will build my Church, and it will withstand the powers of death. I will give you the keys to the kingdom of heaven. Whatever you forbid on earth will be what is forbidden in heaven and whatever you allow on earth will be what is allowed in heaven.'

He gave them strict instructions not to tell anyone that he was Christ. Then he began to explain to them that he was destined to go to Jerusalem and to suffer terribly at the hands of the elders of the Temple, the chief priests and the scribes, and even to be put to death. But that he would rise on the third day.

Drawing Jesus to one side, Simon Peter started to remonstrate with him. 'Heaven preserve you, Lord,' he said, 'this must not happen to you.'

But Jesus rebuked him. 'Get behind me, Satan,' he said. 'Peter you stand in my way when you see things from a man's point of view and not God's.'

Then, addressing all the disciples, he said 'If anyone wants to be a follower of mine, let him give up his life as it is and take up his cross and follow me. For the man who wants to save his life will lose it and the man who loses his life for my sake will find it.

'What good is it for a man to win the whole world if he ruins his life in the process? For if there are those who are ashamed of me and my words, then I will be ashamed of them when I come with the glory of my Father and his angels to reward each one according to his behaviour on earth.'

CHAPTER SEVEN

St. Matthew 17; St. Mark 9; St. Luke 9

The Transfiguration

About a week later Jesus took Simon Peter, James and John up a high mountain to be alone to pray. As Jesus was praying suddenly he was transfigured, his face shone with an extraordinary brilliance and his clothes became as white as the light. Simon Peter and his companions who had been dozing off woke up abruptly when they saw this and as they watched Moses and Elijah appeared on either side of Jesus, talking with him.

At a loss for words, Simon Peter said, 'Lord, it is wonderful for us to be here. Would you like me to make three tents, one for you, one for Moses and one for Elijah?'

But hardly were the words out of his mouth when a bright cloud passed over the sun and plunged them all in shadow, and a voice from behind the cloud said, 'This is my beloved son. Pay attention to his words.'

The disciples fell on their faces, overcome with fear, but Jesus touched them. 'Do not be afraid,' he said. And when they looked up he was alone.

As they walked down the mountain he told them to tell nobody what they had seen until after he, the Son of Man, had risen from the dead. They promised, and kept their promise although they discussed among themselves what Jesus could possibly mean by 'rising from the dead'.

Then they asked him, 'What do the scribes mean when they say that Elijah must come first?'

And he answered, 'Elijah has come already and they did not recognize him but treated him as they pleased. And the Son of Man will suffer in a similar way at their hands.'

And they assumed that he was telling them that John the Baptist had been Elijah.

●

St. Matthew 17; St. Mark 9; St. Luke 9

His Second Warning

Shortly afterwards, when more and more peole were coming to admire Jesus and his work, he reminded his disciples, 'For your part you must bear this fact firmly in your mind, that the Son of Man will be put to death at the hands of man, and three days after his death he will rise again.'

They did not really grasp what he was saying and were embarrassed to ask him. But a great sadness came over them.

●

Jesus Answers: Who is Greatest

One day the disciples were arguing amongst themselves about which of them was the greatest. Jesus knew their thoughts, so he took a little child and sat it beside him, and putting his arms around its shoulders said, 'If anyone wants to be the greatest he must make himself servant of all. Anyone who welcomes a little child like this in my name, welcomes me. And anyone who welcomes me, welcomes the one who sent me.'

Then John said, 'Master we saw a stranger, healing people in your name. Because he was not one of us we tried to stop him.'

And Jesus said, 'Don't stop him. A man who works miracles in my name is not likely to speak evil of me. Anyone who is not against us, is for us.'

Jesus is Stoned

Jesus was in the Temple at Jerusalem for the festival commemorating the rebuilding of that Temple many years before, and the Jews gathered around him and demanded, 'Once and for all tell us plainly if you are the Christ.'

But Jesus replied, 'You know of, and have seen, the things I do in the name of God. Yet still you do not believe.'

The Jews fetched stones to throw at him. Jesus asked them, 'Which of all the things I have done in the name of my Father are you stoning for?'

'We're not stoning you for any of the things you have done,' they replied, 'but for blaspheming. You are a man, and yet you claim to be God.'

They were determined to arrest him and stone him to death, but Jesus escaped from them, and went to the far side of Jordan where John had preached and performed many baptisms.

•

St. John 11–1-44

Lazarus Raised from the Dead

In the village of Bethany there lived a man called Lazarus who had two sisters, Mary and Martha. Jesus knew them well and loved them very much. One day they sent him a message, 'Lord, the man you love is very ill.'

Jesus stayed where he was for two more days, before saying to the disciples, 'We'll go to Judea.'

The disciples thought this unwise for not long before the Jews had tried to stone Jesus to death, and they were worried at the thought of Jesus returning to a place where his enemies wanted to harm him. Jesus said, 'Our friend Lazarus is resting, I am going to wake him.'

The disciples replied, 'If he is resting then surely he will recover.'

But Jesus spoke more plainly. 'Lazarus is dead. But let us go to him.'

So they went. By the time they arrived Lazarus had been dead for four days and was in a tomb. Bethany is not far away from Jerusalem and many Jews from Jerusalem were visiting the sisters to offer their condolences.

Martha hurried out of the house to meet Jesus, and said, 'If you had been here my brother would not have died. But I know that whatever you ask of God, he will give it to you.'

Jesus said, 'Your brother will rise again, Martha . . .'

Martha went into the house and called Mary to see Jesus. Mary got up quickly and went to him, and the Jews who were in the house followed her thinking that

she was going to visit the tomb of Lazarus.

As soon as Mary saw Jesus she threw herself at his feet and said 'Lord, if you had been here, my brother would not have died.'

Seeing her tears, and those of the Jews who followed her, Jesus was very sad and asked, 'Where have you put Lazarus?'

'Come and see,' they replied and Jesus, weeping, followed them. The tomb was a cave with a stone to close the opening.

'Take the stone away,' said Jesus.

Martha said, 'Lord, this is the fourth day. By now the body will smell.'

But Jesus insisted and they removed the stone from the door of the cave.

Then Jesus prayed to God, and called out in a loud voice, 'Lazarus come out.'

And the dead man, his hands and feet bound, his face covered with a cloth, came out.

And Jesus said, 'Unbind him and let him go free.'

●

St. John 11–45-54

Hostility Builds Up

After this, many of the Jews who had witnessed this miracle believed in Jesus, but some reported back to the Pharisees. So the chief priests and Pharisees called a meeting.

'If we let this man carry on in this way everybody will believe in him and the Romans will come and destroy us all. Here he is working all these signs and we're doing nothing about it.'

The High Priest that year was a man called Caiaphas, and he said, 'It's better for one man to die than for the whole nation to be destroyed.'

And from that moment they were determined to kill Jesus, so that he no longer went about openly among the Jews but left the district and went to live in a place on the edge of the desert called Ephraim, where he stayed with his disciples.

•

The Beginning of the Last Journey

The time for Jesus to be taken up to heaven was drawing near and he set out on the road to Jerusalem, sending some of his disciples on ahead. They went into a Samaritan village to make preparations for Jesus to rest there, but the Samaritans, who knew this was a Jewish pilgrimage to Jerusalem, refused to let him into the village.

James and John wanted to punish the Samaritans for their lack of hospitality. 'Let's call down a fire from heaven to burn them up,' they said.

But Jesus scolded them for their spitefulness, and they went to another village.

•

CHAPTER EIGHT

St. Matthew 20; St. Mary 10; St. Luke 18   *St. Matthew 20–20-28, St. Mark 10–35-45*

His Third Warning

As they journeyed to Jerusalem, Jesus told them for a third time what to expect at the end of their journey. They were walking along the hot, dusty road, Jesus striding ahead of them, and he said: 'When we arrive, the Son of Man will be handed over to the chief priests and scribes. They will order him to be put to death. They will hand him over to the non-believers to be mocked and spat upon, whipped until his skin breaks, and crucified. And on the third day he will rise again.'

And although they listened, they had no idea what he was talking about.

The Request

James and John, sons of Zebedee, came with their mother to Jesus. 'We have a request,' they said.

'What is it?' said Jesus.

And they asked for a promise that James and John might sit one at Jesus's left hand, and the other at his right hand in Jesus's kingdom.

'Can you suffer what I am going to suffer?' asked Jesus.

James and John replied, 'We can.'

'Very well,' said Jesus, 'then you shall suffer as I shall. But as for promising you certain seats in heaven, these are not mine to give. They belong to those who have already been given them by my Father.'

When the others heard what James and John had asked for they were indignant about it. Jesus called them all around and he explained: 'You know that in the heathen world, the rulers lord it over everybody else, and have absolute power. But that mustn't be the case among you. No, if you want to be great, you must be prepared to be a servant. The Son of Man has not come to be served, but to serve others. In fact to give his life for them.'

The Man in the Tree

Jesus had to pass through Jericho on his way to Jerusalem. Among the crowd thronging the route to catch a glimpse of Jesus, was a man called Zacchaeus, a wealthy man who was one of the senior tax-collectors.

He was anxious to see Jesus but was too short to see above the heads of the others, so he ran on ahead and climbed a sycamore tree which Jesus would have to pass.

As Jesus reached the place where the sycamore tree was, he stopped and looking up said, 'Zacchaeus, hurry up and come down because I want to stay at your house today.'

Zacchaeus climbed down as swiftly as he could and welcomed Jesus, joyfully. When the bystanders saw the turn of events they grumbled between themselves. 'He has gone to stay at a sinner's house,' they said.

But Zacchaeus said, 'Look sir, I am going to give half of what I have to the poor, and if I have swindled anybody then I am going to repay him four times over.'

And Jesus said, 'Today this house has been saved, because this man is a son of Abraham, and it was the lost that the Son of Man came to find, and to save.'

•

St. Matthew 20; St. Mark 10; St. Luke 18

Blind Bartimaeus

As Jesus was leaving Jericho with his disciples and a large crowd of followers, a blind beggar called Bartimaeus was sitting at the roadside.

Hearing that Jesus was passing by, he began shouting 'Jesus, son of David, have pity on me.'

Many people in the crowd told him to be quiet but the more they scolded the louder he shouted until eventually Jesus heard him and stopped.

'Call him over here,' he said. So they told the blind man 'It's all right now, he's calling you.'

Throwing off his cloak, he stood up and went to Jesus.

'Well,' said Jesus, 'what do you want me to do for you?'

'Master,' said the blind man, 'let me see again.'

Jesus replied, 'Go, your faith has saved you.'

And immediately the blind beggar was no longer blind, and, seeing, he followed Jesus along the road to Jerusalem.

•

St. Matthew 21; St. Mark 11; St. Luke 19

Entry into Jerusalem

They were now drawing very near to Jerusalem and were in fact within sight of Bethphage and Bethany on the Mount of Olives. Jesus sent two of his disciples on ahead and told them, 'Go to that village and you will immediately find a donkey and her colt which has never been ridden, tethered in the street. Untie them and bring them here. If anyone asks you what you are doing, reply that the Master needs them and will send them back later.'

The disciples did as he told them and sure enough found the donkey and the

Down the slope of the Mount of Olives he rode and entered Jerusalem and the whole city was in turmoil. Those who didn't know him were asking the others 'Who is this?' and the reply came, 'This is the prophet Jesus, from Nazareth in Galilee.'

•

St. Luke 19—41-44

Jesus is Moved to Tears

At the sight of the city of Jerusalem, Jesus wept bitterly. 'If you had only known on this day what was necessary for your peace,' he said, 'but you cannot see it. The time is coming when your enemies will surround you and conquer you, destroy your buildings and kill your children and all because you did not recognize your opportunity when God offered it.'

colt tethered as he had described. Just as they were untying them, some men standing nearby asked 'What are you doing?'

'The Master needs them and will send them back directly,' they replied, and the men did not interfere.

They took the donkey and the colt to Jesus and laid their cloaks on the backs of the animals, and Jesus mounted the colt.

As he rode into Jerusalem crowds lined the street and many people threw down their cloaks for him to ride over, and others who had been working in the fields cut great branches from the trees and spread this greenery onto the path before him.

There was tremendous excitement. People were running on ahead, cheering and shouting. 'Hosanna,' they cried. 'God save the Son of David. Blessings on the king who comes in the name of the Lord.'

The Pharisees Complain

Jesus Upsets the Tables of the Temple Traders

Meanwhile Jesus's disciples were still cheering loudly and happily and some Pharisees in the crowd said to Jesus, 'Master, restrain your disciples.'

But he replied, 'I tell you if *they* kept quiet then the very stones in the road would shout out.'

●

He went straight away to the Temple where he was greeted by the usual scene of people buying and selling.

'According to the scripture,' he said, 'My house will be called a house of prayer, but you are turning it into a robber's den.' And with that he upset the tables of the money changers and turned over the chairs of those who were selling sacrificial animals.

There were some blind and lame people in the Temple, and they came to him and he cured them.

'Hosanna,' shouted the children in the Temple. And all this was observed by the chief priests and the scribes and they were afraid of him because of the influence he had over the people, and they tried to find a way of getting rid of him.

●

Jesus at Bethany

And Jesus stayed there all day then in the evening left and spent all night at Bethany, at the house of Lazarus, the man whom he raised from the dead. They gave a dinner in his honour, Lazarus, now competely recovered, sitting at the table and Martha serving the food.

Mary brought out a pound of very costly ointment, prepared from the sweet-smelling plant called Spike-nard. She rubbed it into Jesus's tired feet, wiping them with her hair, until the room was heady with the scent of the ointment.

Judas Iscariot (the traitor amongst Jesus's disciples) said, 'Why wasn't this ointment sold – it's worth at least thirty pounds – and the money used to help the poor?'

(Not that he was particularly fond of the poor, but because he was in charge of the funds Jesus collected and was in the habit of putting some of them in his own pocket.)

But Jesus replied, 'Leave her alone. Let her keep this for my funeral. The poor will always be here . . . but I will not.'

Many Jews came to the house, not only to see Jesus but also to see Lazarus, because they knew he had been raised

from the dead. The chief priests who had already made up their minds to kill Jesus, decided that they might as well kill Lazarus as well because he was the cause of many Jews going over to join Jesus.

CHAPTER NINE

that case why did you refuse to believe him?' And if they said John's baptism came from man, then they would risk offending the many people who believed that John was a prophet.

Instead they replied, 'We do not know the answer.'

'And I,' said Jesus, 'will not tell you my authority for behaving as I do.'

•

St. Matthew 21; St. Mark 11; St. Luke 19

The Confrontation

He went straight away to the Temple and very soon a crowd gathered around him and he began teaching them. The chief priests and the scribes, backed by some other leading citizens, had already discussed how they could get rid of him but their plans were thwarted by the fact that he had such a huge following amongst the population.

On this occasion they decided to confront him and asked him point blank, 'What authority have you for acting like this? Who gave you permission to behave the way you do?'

'First answer one question,' replied Jesus, 'and then I will tell you what you want to know. And this is my question. John's baptism ... did it come from heaven, or from man?'

They argued among themselves what answer they should give him. After all, if they said that John's baptism came from heaven, then Jesus would surely ask, 'In

St. Matthew 22–1-14, St. Luke 14–15-24

Parable of the Wedding Guests

Jesus began to speak to them in parables again. He told them, 'The kingdom of heaven could be compared to a king who gave a great feast for his son's wedding. He sent his servants to fetch the guests but they would not come. So he sent some more servants to remind the guests that he had everything ready for the feast. But still they weren't interested, preferring to go about their own businesses, or attend to their farms. Some even attacked the servants who had brought the invitation, and killed them.

'When the king heard about this he was furious. Summoning his army, he despatched many troops to seek out the murderers, kill them and set fire to their town.

'Then he said to his servants, "The wedding is ready, but as the guests we'd hoped to have turned out to be not good

him out into the darkness. There he can weep and regret his foolishness."

'For many are invited, but few are chosen.'

•

St. Matthew 21; St. Mark 12; St. Luke 20

Parable of the Wicked Servants

He told them another story. 'There was a man who owned land, and planted a vineyard. He fenced it, dug a winepress in it and built a tower. Then he let it to farm-workers and went abroad for a long time. When the time came he sent a servant to collect his share of the vine money from the farm-workers but they attacked the servant and sent him away empty-handed.

'The man sent another servant, this time the farm-workers thrashed him brutally. Then he sent yet another servant and this one they killed, and so they dealt with everyone he sent – wounding some, killing others. Until eventually the man decided to send his only son. "They will surely respect my son," he thought.

'But when the farm-workers saw that it was the son who had come to collect his father's share, they said to each other, "This is the heir. Let's kill him and take over his inheritance."

'And they murdered him and threw his body out of the vineyard.'

Then Jesus asked the people who were listening intently to his every word, 'When the owner of the vineyard comes himself, what will he do to these wicked farm-workers?'

They answered him, 'He will kill the scoundrels, and lease the vineyard to

enough, go instead to the crossroads and invite everyone you see to the wedding."

'So the servants did as they were told and collected an assortment of all sorts of people, good and bad, and the wedding hall was filled with guests.

'Then the king came in to receive the guests and noticed one man who was most unsuitably dressed for a party.

"How did you get in, my friend," he asked the man, "without being properly dressed for a wedding?"

'The man did not reply. Then the king said to the ushers, "Tie him up and throw

The Trick Question

Instead, the Pharisees went away and hatched up a plot between them which they thought would trap Jesus. They sent their disciples with some of Herod's supporters who asked Jesus, 'Master, we know that you are an honest man and that you are not influenced by other people's opinions or approval. Now tell us . . . is it right to pay taxes to Caesar or not?'

But Jesus, seeing through their deceit, said, 'Why try to trap me like this, you hypocrites.' Then he said, 'Let me see the money you pay taxes with.'

So they handed him a silver coin, called a denarius. 'Whose head is this?' asked Jesus, 'what is his name?'

'Why, Caesar's,' they replied.

'In that case,' said Jesus, 'give back to Caesar what belongs to Caesar, and give to God what belongs to God.'

This reply was not at all what they'd expected. They could find no fault with what he said, so they went away.

●

other tenants who will behave properly and give him his share of the proceeds at the right time.'

And Jesus said, 'This is the reason that the kingdom of God is to be taken away from you and given to people who will produce its fruit properly.'

The chief priests and the scribes knew that this parable was aimed at them and they wanted to arrest him but dared not because they were afraid to upset the crowds who regarded Jesus as a leader.

He Answers the Saducees

Then some Saducees (who do not believe in life after death) put this question to Jesus.

They said, 'We are taught that if man dies before he has become a father, then his brother must marry the widow. We know of a case involving seven brothers. The first married and died without children. His brother married the widow, then died before having any children. Then the third brother married her and so on and so on until all seven brothers had been married to the same woman. Then after they had all died, the woman herself died. With life after death, whose wife would she be, having belonged to all of them?'

And Jesus told them, 'Children of this world take husbands and wives, but if they are considered to deserve a place in heaven then they are like angels. There's no marriage in the other world.'

•

He Answers the Pharisees

This remark silenced the Saducees, so then the Pharisees asked him a question.

'Master,' they said, 'which is the most important of all the commandments?'

And Jesus replied, 'The most important commandment is that you shall love the Lord your God with all your heart, with all your soul and with all your mind. And after that the next most important commandment is to love your neighbour as you love yourself.'

False Scribes

While all the people were still listening intently, he changed the subject and said to his disciples, 'Be on your guard against the scribes who like walking around in flowing robes, and having people bow to them in public, take the front seats at the synagogue and the best places at dinner parties. They profit from the property of widows and cover up themselves with lengthy prayers. These men are heading for severe punishment.'

•

The Widow's Mite

The End of the Temple

All this time people were coming in, putting their offerings into the collecting box. Some rich people put in a great deal but Jesus noticed a poor widow drop in two small coins, worth about a penny, and he said, 'I tell you truly that this poor widow has put in more than any of the others. For they have given what they could easily afford to give, but she has given everything she has.'

As he was leaving the Temple, one of his disciples drew Jesus's attention to the building itself. 'Look at the size of these stones, Master. How enormous they are.'

And Jesus replied, 'You see these great buildings? Not a single stone will remain, everything will be destroyed.'

'When will this happen,' they asked him. 'What will be the sign that the end of the world is coming?'

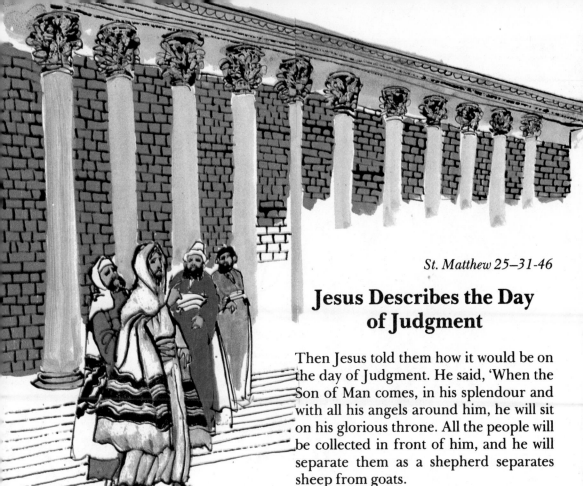

Jesus Describes the Day of Judgment

Then Jesus told them how it would be on the day of Judgment. He said, 'When the Son of Man comes, in his splendour and with all his angels around him, he will sit on his glorious throne. All the people will be collected in front of him, and he will separate them as a shepherd separates sheep from goats.

'He will place the sheep on his right-hand side, the goats on his left-hand side. Then he will say to those on his right, "Come you who have earned my Father's blessing. This kingdom has been kept for you since the beginning of time. For I was hungry and you gave me food. I was thirsty and you gave me a drink. I was lonely and you gave me friendship. I was naked and you gave me clothes. I was ill and you cared for me. I was in prison and you came to see me there."

'Then these honest people will say to him, "Lord, when did all this happen?" And the king will answer, "I assure you that by doing this for the least important of my brothers, you did it for me."

'Then, turning to those on his left-hand side he will say, "Go away from me,

And Jesus told them, 'The sun will be darkened. The moon will lose its brightness. The stars will fall out of the sky and the heavens will shake. And the Son of Man will appear in the clouds, strong and glorious and he will send his angels to every corner of the earth to fetch the ones he has chosen to be with him in heaven.

'Be on your guard and stay awake, for if he comes unexpectedly he mustn't find you asleep.'

●

249

you who have been cursed, go into the fire which is blazing for the Devil and his angels! For I was starving and you gave me nothing to eat. I was thirsty and you gave me nothing to drink. I was a stranger and you never welcomed me. I was naked and you gave me no clothes. I was sick and in prison and you never visited me."

'And they, in their turn will ask, "But Lord when did we see *you* like this?" And he will reply, "I assure you that by neglecting to help the humblest of my brothers, you neglected to do it for me."

'And they will suffer punishment for ever. And the good will enjoy life for ever.'

•

St. Luke 21—37-38

Jesus Waits

As the feast of the Passover drew near, Jesus waited, spending his nights on the hill called Mount of Olives, and his days in the Temple, talking to the people who gathered eagerly around him.

CHAPTER TEN

St. Matthew 26; St. Mark 14; St. Luke 22

The Plotters

Meanwhile the chief priests and senior citizens were discussing a way of getting rid of Jesus. They met in the place of the High Priest, whose name was Caiaphas, and planned how to have Jesus arrested by some trick and then killed. And they agreed on one thing, 'It must not happen during the festivities for that could cause a riot amongst the people.'

•

St. Matthew 26—1-2

The End Draws Near

Two days before the feast, and having finished all his teaching, Jesus called his disciples around him and told them, 'As you know it will be Passover in two days time, and the Son of Man is going to be betrayed, and crucified.'

•

Plans for the Passover

When the time of the Passover feast came, the disciples asked Jesus, 'Where do you want us to eat the Passover supper?'

And he said to Simon Peter and John, 'Listen, as you go into the city you will see a man carrying a jug of water. Follow him and he will go into a house. Go into the house and say to the owner, 'The Master says where is the room in which I can eat Passover with my disciples?' He will take you upstairs to a large room furnished with couches, and prepared for the supper. Make arrangements for us to eat there.'

They set off and found everything just as he had said it would be, and prepared the Passover.

•

St. Matthew 26; St. Mark 14; St. Luke 22

The Betrayer

Then Judas Iscariot, one of the disciples, went to the Temple police with a plan for handing Jesus over to them. They were delighted. 'What will you give me in return?' he asked, and they handed over thirty pieces of silver on the spot. From that moment Judas Iscariot waited for the right time to betray Jesus, without the people knowing about it.

•

St. Matthew 26; St. Luke 22; St. Mark 14; St. John 13

The Last Supper

The time came for supper, and Jesus sat down at the table with his disciples. 'I have waited to eat this meal with you,' he said, 'for now it is time for me to suffer and believe me, I shall not eat the Passover again until all that it really means is fulfilled in the kingdom of God.'

Then Jesus got up from the table, took off his robe and tied a towel around his waist. Then he poured water into a basin and kneeling began to wash his disciples' feet, and to wipe them with the towel.

When he, came to Simon Peter, the disciple asked, 'Surely you aren't going to

wash my feet?' And Jesus answered, 'At the moment you do not quite understand what I am doing. Later you will.

When he had finished, he put his clothes on again and went back to his place at the table and said, 'Do you understand what I have done? You call me teacher and Lord which is right for I am. If I, as Lord and teacher, can wash your feet, this is an example to you, and you must be ready to do the same for each other.'

Then he took some bread and, after saying grace, broke the bread into pieces and gave a piece to each at the table, and said, 'This is my body, take it. Do this in memory of me.'

Then, taking a cup of wine, he passed it to each of them saying, 'This is my blood which will be poured for you. I tell you truly that I shall drink no more wine until the day I drink the new wine with you in the kingdom of heaven.'

And then he said, 'There is someone sitting at this table who is going to betray me.' They were all very distressed at this. 'Not I, Lord,' they said, each in turn – including Judas Iscariot.

•

St. John 13–21-30

Jesus Predicts the Betrayal

Jesus repeated, 'I assure you one of you will betray me.'

The disciples looked at each other, wondering whom he could possibly mean. John, the disciple Jesus loved most of all, was reclining on the couch beside him and Simon Peter said to John, 'Ask him which of us he means.'

And John, leaning towards Jesus, asked 'Who is it, Lord?'

And Jesus said, 'It is the one to whom I shall now give this piece of bread,' and with that he handed a piece of bread to Judas Iscariot. Then Jesus said to Judas Iscariot, 'What you are going to do, do it quickly.'

None of the others knew what he meant. They thought that, because Judas looked after their funds, Jesus was telling him to go out and buy something or else to give something to the poor.

As soon as Judas had taken the bread, he got up from the table and went outside into the night.

•

St..Matthew 26; St. Mark 14; St. Luke 22; St. John 13

The Disciples' Promise

They sang psalms then left the house, walking to the Mount of Olives. On the way there Jesus told them, 'Before the night is over, you will lose faith in me.' Turning to Simon Peter he said, 'I have prayed for you so that your faith may not fail, and once you have recovered you in turn must strengthen your brothers.'

Simon Peter said, 'Even if all lose faith in you, I would not. I would be ready to go to prison with you. I will lay down my life for you.'

'Lay down your life for me?' answered Jesus, 'I tell you before the cock crows today you will have denied three times that you even know me.'

'If I have to die with you I will never disown you,' said Simon Peter and all the disciples said the same.

St. John 14–1-10

Jesus Talks of God

Then Jesus said, 'Don't be upset. Trust God and trust me. My father's house has many rooms and I am going to get a place ready for you, and I shall return and take you with me so that we can be together. You know where I am going, and you know the road I am going to take.'

Thomas said, 'Lord, we don't know where you are going, so how can we know the road you are going to take?'

Jesus replied, 'I, myself, am that road and the truth and the life. No one approaches the Father except through me.'

Philip said, 'Lord, let us see the Father and then we shall be satisfied.'

'Have I been with you all this time,' said Jesus, 'without your really knowing me? If you've seen me, you have seen the Father.'

St. Matthew 26; St. Mark 14; St. Luke 22

Jesus Prays Alone

They came to a vine-grove called Gethsemane on the Mount of Olives. 'Pray that you won't have to be put to the test,' he told them. Then he walked a short distance away, leaving the disciples except for Simon Peter, and the sons of Zebedee who went with him. He seemed overwhelmed with sadness. 'My heart is almost breaking,' he said. 'Wait here and keep awake with me.' Then he went on a little farther alone and, kneeling on the ground, prayed.

He came back to the disciples and found them sleeping.

'Can't you keep awake with me for one hour?' he asked. A second time he went away and prayed, and came back to find that again they had fallen asleep. Leaving them, he went away and prayed for a third time.

He returned and said to them, 'Now you can sleep. It is all over. The time has come for the Son of Man to be betrayed into the hands of evil men. Look, here comes my betrayer.'

•

St. Matthew 26; St. Mark 14; St. Luke 22; St. John 18

The Arrest

At that moment they were surrounded by Roman soldiers and Temple police, armed with torches and weapons and carrying lanterns. At their head was Judas Iscariot, who knew where to find Jesus because the garden was a favourite place of his. Judas had already arranged with the soldiers to identify Jesus by kissing him.

'Greetings, teacher,' he said and kissed Jesus.

'Judas,' said Jesus, 'are you betraying the Son of Man with a kiss? My friend, then get on with it and do what you came for.'

Then he stepped forward. 'Who are you looking for?' he asked the soldiers.

'Jesus of Nazareth,' they said.

He said, 'I am Jesus.' They took a step back, and again he asked them 'Who are you looking for?'

'Jesus,' they replied.

'I have told you, I am he,' said Jesus. 'I am the one you are looking for. Let these others go.'

As the soldiers went to seize Jesus his disciples said 'Lord, shall we use our swords?' Simon Peter drew his sword and wounded the high priest's servant, Malchus, cutting off his right ear. Jesus said, 'Put your sword back.' And touching the man's ear, healed it.

Then, speaking to the soldiers, he said, 'Am I a criminal that you had to come for me armed with swords and clubs. I have been sitting among you in the Temple for days and you never attempted to lay hands on me then.'

Then they seized Jesus but his disciples turned and ran away. The soldiers grabbed at one of them, who was wearing a loose linen robe, catching hold of the cloth but he slipped out of it and escaped, naked.

St. Matthew 26; St. Mark 14; St. Luke 23; St. John 18

Trial at Night

The Roman soldiers and the Jewish guards bound Jesus and took him to Caiaphas the High Priest where the scribes and elders were gathered together. Simon Peter followed at a distance and when the crowd reached the

The High Priest then asked Jesus, 'Do you have anything to say to that?'

Jesus was silent.

Caiaphas said, 'Tell us if you are Christ the Son of God.'

'I am,' said Jesus.

At this the High Priest cried, 'Blasphemy. We do not need any further witnesses. You've all heard the blasphemy . . .what is your verdict?'

And everybody shouted. 'He deserves to die.'

They blindfolded him and spat in his face and hit him. 'Who was that who hit you, Christ.' they mocked. 'Prophesy that!'

priest's palace, Simon Peter went in and sat with the servants to see what would be the outcome.

The priests and the Sanhedrin (which was the Jewish court of law) were looking for evidence, even if it was false evidence, which would give them an excuse to condemn Jesus to death.

Several lying witnesses came forward but their evidence wasn't strong enough. Then two men stepped forward and said that Jesus had told them he had the power to destroy the Temple and rebuild it in three days.

St. Matthew 26; St. Mark 15; St. Luke 23; St. John 18

Simon Peter's Denial

Whilst Jesus was being questioned, Simon Peter was sitting outside in the courtyard, warming himself by the fire. A servant girl saw him, 'You, too, were with Jesus,' she said.

'I don't know what you're talking about,' said Simon Peter. He moved away from the fire and presently another servant approached him, a relative of the man whose ear Simon Peter had cut off.

'You too were with Jesus of Nazareth,' he said.

'I don't even know the man,' said Simon Peter.

Then some bystanders said, 'You are one of them for sure, your accent gives you away.'

Then Simon Peter began cursing them and shouting 'I don't know the man.'

At that moment there was a sound of a cock crowing and Simon Peter remembered that Jesus had told him, 'Before the cock crows you will deny me three times.'

Then Simon Peter went outside, and broke down and sobbed bitterly.

•

St. Matthew 27; St. Mark 15; St. Luke 23; St. John 18, 19

Sentenced to Death

Dawn came and all the Jewish assembly marched with Jesus to Pontius Pilate (the Roman Governor) to make their complaints against him.

'This man has been corrupting the people, telling them it is wrong to pay taxes to Caesar, claiming that he is Christ, a king,' they said.

Pilate turned to Jesus, 'Are you the King of the Jews?' he asked.

'Yes, I am a king,' said Jesus, 'But my kingdom is not of this world. If it were, my men could have fought for me.'

'I can't find anything *criminal* about this man,' said Pilate to the chief priests and the crowd.

But they weren't satisfied and insisted ... 'He is a troublemaker with his teachings, all the way through Judea from Galilee to this place.'

Hearing this Pilate realized that, as a Galilean, Jesus came under Herod's rule, and as Herod happened to be in Jerusalem at that time, Pilate passed Jesus over to Herod.

Herod was pleased to see Jesus, because he had heard a lot about him and had been hoping to see him with his own eyes. He was also hoping that he might see Jesus perform some miracle, so, while the chief priests and scribes gathered outside, he questioned him at length but Jesus did not reply to his questions.

Herod and his guards made fun of Jesus, even to the extent of putting a rich ceremonial cloak on him, and then they sent him back to Pilate.

who was in prison for murder and causing a riot).

Pilate realized that it was out of jealousy that the priests and scribes were against Jesus. Also during the day his wife had sent him a message warning him to have nothing to do with the death of Jesus. 'I have been upset by a dream I had about him,' she said. Pilate didn't want to get too involved with the affair.

'What am I to do with this man who is King of the Jews?' he asked, and they screamed with one voice: 'CRUCIFY HIM. CRUCIFY HIM.'

Pilate could see that the crowd was in a dangerous state. He called for some water and, in front of the crowd, washed his hands saying 'I am innocent of this man's blood. It's your affair.'

Then he ordered Barabbas to be set free, and he ordered Jesus to be whipped, then handed over for crucifixion.

•

St. Matthew 27–3-10

Judas' Remorse

When Judas heard that Jesus had been condemned to death, he was overcome with remorse and went back to the chief priest and the elders taking the thirty pieces of silver.

'I have done wrong,' he said, 'I have betrayed an innocent man.'

'That's your business,' they said. 'It's no concern of ours.'

He threw down the money, went out and hanged himself. The chief priests picked up the money but agreed that they couldn't put it back into the Temple funds because it was blood-money, so they used it to buy a field as a burial place for foreigners.

Pilate called the chief priests and the leading men and the people and said, 'You brought this man to me, telling me he was a troublemaker, and I've gone into the matter and I can find no proof against him. Neither can Herod, for he has sent him back to us. Since the man has done nothing to deserve death, I'll have him whipped, then set him free.'

It was the custom to release a prisoner at Passover time so this would have been quite in order. But the crowd shrieked, 'No. Set free Barabbas.' (This was a man

CHAPTER ELEVEN

St. Matthew 27–27-31, St. Mark 15–16-20

Mockery

The soldiers took Jesus to the inner part of the palace called the Praetorium. They dressed him in a fine purple robe and twisted some thorns into a crown and put that on his head. They put a reed into his hand, and making fun of him knelt saying, 'Hail, King of the Jews.' Then they took the reed out of his hand and hit him on the head with it. Finally they took off the fine purple robe, dressed him in his own clothes and led him away to be crucified.

●

St. Matthew 27; St. Mark 15; St. Luke 23;
St. John 19

The Crucifixion

The place for the crucifixion was called Golgotha (which means place of skulls) and on the way there they came across a traveller called Simon from Cyrene, and asked him to help carry Jesus's cross. There were two others to be crucified with Jesus that day, one on either side of him. Pilate wrote out a notice and had it fixed to Jesus's cross. It said: This is Jesus, The King of the Jews.

The writing was in Hebrew, Latin and Greek. The Jewish chief priests objected to the words used.'You shouldn't write: *King of the Jews*, but: *This man said, "I am King of the Jews"*' they said.

But Pilate answered, 'It's written and that's that.' They offered Jesus wine mixed with myrrh which he tasted but refused to drink.

When the soldiers had finished nailing Jesus to the cross they divided his clothing into four shares, one for each of them. His undergarment was in one piece, and since they didn't want to tear it they threw dice to see who should have it.

'Father, forgive them, they do not know what they are doing,' said Jesus.

The crowd jeered at him. 'You said you could rebuild the Temple in three days, how about saving yourself and come down from the cross,' they shouted.

'He saved others yet he cannot save himself,' said the priests and scribes.

'If you're the Son of God, let God rescue you,' cried others.

One of the criminals, hanging beside him, said, 'If you're Christ, save yourself and us as well.'

But the other spoke up. 'We deserved our sentence,' he said, 'Jesus has done nothing to deserve it. Jesus, will you remember me when you come into your kingdom?'

'I promise you,' Jesus replied, 'that today you will be with me in paradise.'

Then the sun was covered, and it was very dark and this lasted for three hours. Near the cross stood Jesus's mother, and his mother's sister Mary the wife of Clopas, and Mary Magdalene. Seeing his mother and the disciple, John, whom he loved, standing near to her, Jesus said to his mother 'Woman, this is your son.' And to the disciple he said, 'This is your mother.'

Then those standing near to the cross heard him cry, 'My God, my God, why have you deserted me?'

Somebody ran and soaked a sponge in rough wine and putting it on the end of a reed stretched it out and held it to his mouth.

After he had drunk it, Jesus said, 'It is accomplished.' His head fell forward and he died.

At this precise moment the veil of the Temple was torn in two, and there was an earthquake. The Roman soldier who was guarding Jesus said: 'Truly, this was the Son of God.'

In accordance with the custom, the soldiers came to break the legs of the men who had been crucified. They broke the legs of one man, then the other, but when they came to Jesus they saw that he was dead, and so, instead of breaking his legs, one of the soldiers pierced his side with a sword and immediately there came out blood and water.

Many of his friends stood at a distance, including the women who had come with him from Galilee, and they saw all this happen.

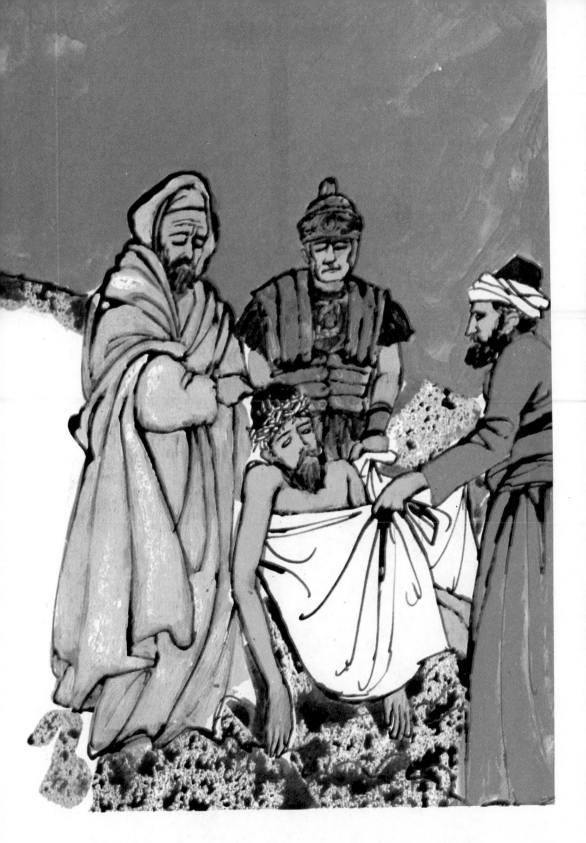

The Burial

Then a member of the Jewish council who had secretly been a disciple of Jesus arrived. His name was Joseph and he came from Arimathaea, a Jewish town. He had not agreed with what the others had done to Jesus and now he went to Pilate and asked for the body of Jesus. Pilate, astonished that Jesus should have died so quickly, sent for the soldiers to ask if he was already dead. When they assured him that Jesus was dead, Pilate told Joseph he could take the body, and Joseph then took the body down off the cross. He wrapped it in a clean linen cloth with spices, following the Jewish burial custom and laid Jesus in a tomb which had been cut out of the rock.

Then Joseph put a huge stone at the opening of the tomb, and went away as it was the beginning of the Sabbath.

The women who had been with Jesus, watched where Joseph put the body then they went away and prepared spices and ointments.

•

The Guard

The following day the chief priests and Pharisees went to Pilate because they were worried that Jesus had said, 'After three days I shall rise again.' They were afraid that his disciples might steal the body and then tell the people that Jesus had indeed risen from the dead. They wanted permission to place a guard near the tomb to make sure that this did not happen.

Pilate said, 'You may have your guard.' So they went and made sure that the entrance to the tomb was secure, and left several Temple soldiers guarding it.

CHAPTER TWELVE

St. Matthew 28; St. Mark 16; St. Luke 24;
St. John 20

The Resurrection

On the morning of the following day, it was still quite dark, and Mary Magdalene went to the tomb. She saw that the stone had been moved away from the tomb, and ran back to Simon Peter and John.

'They have taken Jesus, and I don't know where he is,' she said. Both disciples hurried to the tomb. They saw the linen clothes lying on the ground, and Simon Peter went right into the tomb and saw the cloth that had been over Jesus's head. They understood then that Jesus had risen from the dead. They went home. But Mary remained there, weeping. After a while, she stooped to look inside and saw two angels dressed in white. They were sitting where the body of Jesus had been, one at the head and one at the feet.

'Why are you crying?' they asked her.

'Because they have taken my Lord away and I don't know where they have put him,' she said. As she said this she turned and saw another man standing there. It was Jesus, but she did not at first recognize him.

'Why are you weeping? Who are you looking for?' he asked her.

Mary thought he must be the gardener. 'Sir, if you have taken him away, please tell me where he is.'

Jesus said, simply, 'Mary.' And then she knew him.

'Master,' she said, overjoyed.

Jesus said to her, 'Do not cling to me. I have not yet ascended to my Father. But go and find the brothers, and tell them that I am soon to go up to my Father, your Father. My God who is your God. And tell my brothers they must leave for Galilee. I will see them there.'

Mary did as Jesus told her.

Mary told her story, but at the time it seemed pure nonsense and very difficult to believe.

●

St. Mark 16–12-13, St. Luke 24–13-35

The Stranger on the Road to Emmaus

That same day two of the disciples were on the way to a village called Emmaus some miles outside Jerusalem. Of course they could talk of nothing but the events of the past few days. As they were walking, engrossed in their conversation a man joined them. They thought it was a stranger but in fact it was Jesus and they didn't recognize him.

'What are you talking about?' he asked them. They stopped at once, their faces sorrowful.

The one called Cleopas answered, 'You must be the only person for miles around who doesn't know what's been going on in Jerusalem the last few days,' he said.

'Oh, what's that?' asked Jesus.

'Why, all the things concerning Jesus of Nazareth,' said Cleopas, still not recognizing that it was Jesus he was talking to. 'Jesus the one who was a great leader. We had all hoped that he would be the one to lead Israel to freedom, but our chief priests and scribes had him crucified. The crucifixion happened two whole days ago, and now we are all astonished by some women from our group who went to the tomb to find him gone. And they say that the angels told them he is still alive. Some of our friends also looked into the tomb, and he was gone.'

'What foolish men you are,' said Jesus, and began to explain to them all the passages from the scriptures which referred to Jesus. They were still talking when they arrived at the village, and the two

disciples insisted that Jesus should spend the evening with them, and he agreed.

They sat down to supper together, and Jesus took the bread and broke it and handed them each a piece. With this simple act they suddenly realized who he was, and, at that moment of recognition, he disappeared.

Immediately they hurried back to Jerusalem to report to the others, only to hear that meanwhile Jesus had appeared to Simon Peter.

•

St. Mark 16; St. Luke 24; St. John 20

Jesus Returns

They were still talking about all this, in a room with locked doors for they were afraid of the Jews, when Jesus appeared standing with them. Alarmed and frightened they thought they were seeing a ghost.

'Peace be with you,' said Jesus. 'Why are you so worried. Look at the marks on my hands and feet . . . you can see it is I. Touch me if you wish . . . I am flesh and bones, nothing ghostlike at all.'

Then they were so overjoyed that they were speechless.

•

St. John 20–24-29

Thomas is Convinced

Thomas, one of the disciples, was not with them when all this happened, and later when the others told him about it he was disbelieving.

'Unless I can see with my own eyes the

are my hands,' and he showed him the marks of the nails. Then taking Thomas's hand he said, 'Look, here is the hole in my side. Put your hand there and feel for yourself.

'Don't have any more doubts. Believe what you see.'

Thomas, knowing that this was indeed Jesus, said, 'Teacher, my God.'

And Jesus said, 'Yes, now you believe because you can see me. It's even better to be one of those who has not seen yet can still believe.'

•

St. John 21–1-14

The Stranger on the Beach

Some days later the disciples were fishing by Lake Tiberias. They had been fishing all night without having caught a thing. As it grew light, they were aware of a

holes where the nails went into his hands and feet, and touch with my own hand the hole in his side where they pierced him, then I refuse to believe what you say,' said Thomas.

Eight days later the disciples were again together in the house, and this time Thomas was with them. The doors were closed, but suddenly Jesus stood among them.

'Peace be with you,' he said. Then, turning to Thomas, he said, 'Look, here

They dragged the net ashore marvelling that, although it was full of big fish, it was not broken. Jesus shared the bread and the fish he'd cooked among them.

None of the disciples was bold enough to ask, 'Who are you.' But they knew without asking that it was Jesus.

•

St. Matthew 28; St. Mark 16; St. Luke 24

The Ascension

Jesus visited them once more. They were together in a room and he led them as far as the outskirts of Bethany, to a high place, and he blessed them all. And then he told them, 'Go out into the world and tell the good news to everyone. Find new followers in every country and teach them what I have taught you, and know that I shall be with you always, to the end of time.' And after this he walked a few paces away and stood by himself and, standing there, was carried up to heaven.

His disciples watched, then, full of happiness and hope they turned and took the road back to Jerusalem.

man standing on the shore, but they didn't know who it was.

'Have you had a good catch, friend?' called out the man. 'No,' they replied.

'Cast the net again, and you'll find something,' said the man. So they dropped the net, which was immediately so heavy with fish that they couldn't haul it in.

'It is the Lord,' said John, realizing that the man was in fact Jesus.

At this they all started scrambling about to get the boat and fish onto land, and as they came ashore they saw that there was a small meal prepared of bread, and fish cooking over a charcoal fire.

'Come and have breakfast,' said Jesus, 'and bring some of the fish you have just caught.'

THE ACTS OF THE APOSTLES

The Beginning of the Church in Jerusalem

It was the day of Pentecost, a harvest festival, and Jesus's apostles, who were in the habit of meeting daily, were in a room together. Peter and John, James and Andrew, Philip and Thomas, Bartholomew and Matthew, James son of Alphaeus and Simon the Zealot, and Jude son of James, and also Matthias who had been selected to take the place of Judas Iscariot.

Suddenly the entire house was filled with the sound of rushing wind, and tongues of fire licked into the room and, separating, came to rest on the head of each man. Immediately they began speaking to each other in foreign languages, and understanding each other.

In Jerusalem at that time were many religious men from other countries and they quickly gathered at the house and to their astonishment each heard his own language being spoken. Parthians, Medes, Mesopotamians, Elamites, Asians, Egyptians, Libians, Romans, Cretans, men from Judea, Cappadocia, Pontus and Phrygia and Pamphylia ... all listened in amazement to these men whom they knew to be Galileans speaking in other tongues. They could find no explanation for this.

A few tried to laugh it off. 'They're drunk,' they declared, but Peter corrected them. 'Hardly drunk,' he said, 'at nine o'clock in the morning.'

Then Peter talked to the people about Jesus and his crucifixion and as they listened they were deeply touched. Throughout the day more than three thousand people came forward to be baptised.

These were the first Christians. They set up their own community, sold their possessions and shared the money between themselves providing for each according to his needs. They went to the Temple every day to pray, and met in each other's houses to break bread as Jesus had done at the last supper.

People admired them for their kindness and generosity, and the miracles worked through the apostles aroused great interest, so that each day more people joined them.

●

Cure of the Lame Beggar

There was a forty-year-old man who had been crippled from birth, who spent his days sitting begging at the Beautiful Gate near the Temple. One day as Peter and John were on their way to the Temple they passed this beggar who was being carried by his relatives. Seeing them he held out his hand to beg for something, but Peter said 'I have no money but I will give you what I have. In the name of Jesus, walk.' And he took the beggar's hand and helped him to stand up. As he did so the cripple's feet and ankles became strong and he began to walk and jump about. Then still clinging to Peter and John he went with them to the Temple recognised by everybody as the beggar who used to sit at the Beautiful Gate, and the people talked among themselves but could find no possible explanation for this miraculous cure.

●

The Deception of Ananias and Sapphira

The apostles were frequently in trouble with priests at the Temple for continuous talking of Christ's resurrection. At the same time their fame spread, attracting more people to join them. Although they had no possessions, they were never in need, for people gave them money, often selling their land or houses in order to raise money to give.

There was a man called Ananias who agreed to sell some property and give the money to the apostles. But having sold it he couldn't quite bring himself to part with all the money so he and his wife Sapphira agreed to keep some of it back and pretend it had fetched a smaller price.

When he gave the money to the apostles, Peter said: 'The land was yours. When you had sold it the money was yours. Why should you lie? You have lied to God.' At this Ananias fell dead to the ground.

The people watching were shocked and some of the younger men carried the body away to be buried. Some hours later Sapphira came in, unaware of what had happened. Peter challenged her: 'Was this the price you got for your land?' he asked. 'Yes' she replied.

'So you thought you could trick God,' said Peter. 'What made you do such a thing?' The sound of footsteps could be heard outside.

'Do you hear that?' said Peter 'they have been to bury your husband, they will bury you too.'

At that Sapphira fell dead at his feet and the young men took her and buried her beside her husband.

•

Acts 9–36-43

The Dead Woman Raised to Life

The apostles worked many miracles. One day one of the disciples, a woman called Tabitha (sometimes known as Dorcas) of Jaffa was taken ill and died. She was a very good woman, who spent her days

caring for others, and the disciples who lived with her washed her body and laid it in an upstairs room. Then, having heard that Peter was in the neighbouring town of Lydda, they sent for him.

He came at once and went to the room where the body of Tabitha lay, surrounded by her friends and women weeping, showing him the beautiful needlework Tabitha had sewn when she was alive. Peter sent them out of the room, then knelt by the body and prayed. After this he looked straight at the body and said 'Get up, Tabitha.'

And she opened her eyes and sat up, and he gave her his hand and helped her to her feet. Then he called the disciples and showed them that Tabitha was alive again.

•

Acts 6–8

Stephen is Stoned to Death

Stephen, one of the apostles, began to work many miracles and when people from the synagogue came forward to argue with him they found they couldn't fault his wisdom. So they bribed some men to say that they had heard Stephen using blasphemous language. Then they had him arrested and brought before the Sanhedrin.

Stephen tried to persuade the members of the council that what he said and did in the name of Jesus was right, but everything he said made them more angry.

Suddenly Stephen looked up into the sky and saw God with Jesus standing on his right.

'I can see Heaven wide open,' he told

the council, 'with Jesus standing at God's right hand.'

This enraged the members of the council. They blocked their ears with their hands and shouted at him, then they dragged him outside the city wall and stoned him.

It was hot and some of them took off their clothes and put them at the feet of a young man called Paul (sometimes known as Saul) so that he could mind them. Paul watched the death of Stephen, entirely approving of the stoning.

That was the beginning of a bitter persecution against the Christians and many of them had to run away for their safety to the country districts of Judea and Samaria where they spread the teachings of Jesus. Meanwhile Paul was working to destroy the Church of Jerusalem and went from house to house looking for Christians whom he arrested and sent to prison.

•

Acts 9–1-19

Paul's Conversion

He was so intent on killing Jesus's disciples that he even asked the high priest to give him a letter of introduction to the synagogues in Damascus, authorising him to arrest any Christians, men or women, he could find there and fetch them back to Jerusalem.

On the road to Damascus just outside the city, he was suddenly halted by a brilliant light all around him. It was such a shock that he fell to the ground and then he heard a voice say: 'Saul, Saul why are you persecuting me?'

'Who are you, Lord?' asked Paul, and the voice replied 'I am Jesus, and you are persecuting me. Get up, and go to Damascus and there you will be told what you must do.'

The men travelling with him were speechless for although they had seen the dazzling brilliance and heard the voice they could see no one. The light went, and Paul groped his way to his feet, for even with his eyes wide open, he could see nothing.

His companions led him by the hand into Damascus. Meanwhile a disciple called Ananias who lived in Damascus had a vision in which Jesus told him to go to Paul. 'You will find him in the house of Judas in Straight Street, Damascus,' said Jesus. 'He is Saul of Tarsus, he is praying, having had a vision of a man called Ananias coming in and laying hands on him to restore his sight.'

At this Ananias replied: 'Lord, I've heard of this man, and I know all about the harm he has been doing to your disciples in Jerusalem. I know too that he has come here with a warrant to arrest everybody who acts in your name.'

'Nevertheless I have chosen him to

281

But the disciples found out about the plot and when it was dark they put Paul in a basket and lowered him from the top of the wall. He returned to Jerusalem, to join the disciples there. At first they were wary of him, remembering his past record, but Barnabas intervened, telling them about Paul's vision on the road to Damascus and of the work he had done in Damascus. After this he began working with the disciples, until they found out about a plot to kill him, and they sent him away to Tarsus for safety.

•

Acts 15–36-41, Acts 16–1-10

Paul's Travels

One day whilst they were praying Paul and Barnabas were told by God that he wanted them to set off on the work for which he had called them and they went to preach the story of Jesus, in foreign lands. They travelled far, but later they quarrelled and each went his own way. Then Paul chose Silas to be his companion, and continued his missionary work.

They travelled through Syria and Cilcia, Derbe and Lystra, strengthening the faith of the churches and establishing new ones. They passed through Phrygia and Galatia, having been instructed not to preach there, through Mysia and Troas.

One night Paul had a vision in which a man said: 'Come to Macedonia to help us.' He lost no time in arranging to go to Macedonia, convinced that this was a message from God.

•

work for me,' replied the Lord. 'You must go and do as I say.'

So Ananias went to the house and found Paul there, and touched him, saying 'Brother Saul, I have come from Jesus to restore your sight, so that you will be filled with the Holy Spirit.'

And at once it was as if scales had fallen from his eyes and Paul could see again. They baptised him, and then he was given food, for he had not eaten for three days.

•

Acts 9–20-30

Escape in a Basket

He stayed with the disciples in Damascus for a few days and then began at once preaching in the synagogues and telling the people that Jesus was the son of God. Those who heard him were amazed, for it was common knowldge that he was the man who had come from Jerusalem expressly to arrest Christians.

The Jews at Damascus were quite confused by this and also by the things he said and, after a time they worked out a plot to kill him, keeping watch on the city gates so that he could not escape.

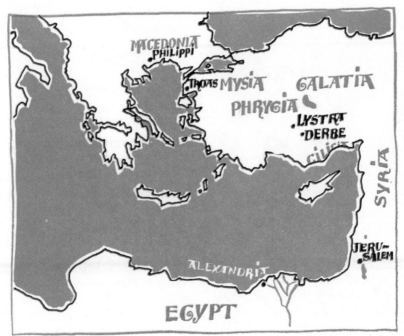

Acts 16–11-40

Imprisonment and Deliverance

They stayed at Philippi, one of the main cities in Macedonia, and one day as they were going to pray they met a slave girl who told people's fortunes. Immediately she tagged on to them shouting 'These men are God's servants. They have come to show us how to be saved.'

Each day she repeated this until eventually Paul became irritated and turning, said 'I order you to leave that woman,' and the evil spirit left her and she was quiet. Her masters, who profited by her fortune telling now had no further chance of making money out of her and they were very angry. They seized Paul and Silas and dragged them to the market place, before the magistrates.

They charged Paul and Silas 'These men are causing a disturbance.' The crowd shouted agreement, and the magistrates ordered Paul and Silas to be stripped of their clothes and whipped, then they were thrown into prison.

The goaler, who had been warned to keep a close watch on them, put them into the innermost cell, with their feet secured in stocks.

Night came, and as Paul and Silas were praying and singing hymns, there was a sudden earthquake that shook the very foundations of the prison. The doors flew open, the prisoners' chains fell from them.

The goaler, wakened by the noise, saw the doors open and drew his sword to kill himself, sooner than await punishment for letting his prisoners escape. But Paul shouted to him. 'Don't harm yourself, we are all here.'

The goaler rushed in with lights to see for himself, and realizing that they must be men of God was very frightened.

'What must I do to be saved?' he asked them and they told him, 'Become a

283

Paul the Captive

Paul was in the Temple in Jerusalem when some Jews who were against him started shouting, 'This is the man who has been going around preaching against us.' People came running and the mob, whipped up into a frenzy, dragged Paul out of the Temple and beat him. He was within inches of losing his life, but soldiers at a Roman garrison nearby heard the pandemonium and men were sent at once to quell the riot.

Paul was arrested and put in chains. It was impossible to question him on the spot because of the noise of the crowd, so the soldiers carried him to the fort. They were under the impression that they had captured an Egyptian who was wanted for having organized a revolt, but when Paul spoke to them in Greek they realized their mistake.

He asked permission to talk to the crowd and standing at the top of the stairs he spoke to them in Hebrew. He told them of his earlier life when he had persecuted the Christians, of the men and women he had sent chained to prison and death. He told them what had happened to him on the road to Damascus, of his blindness and how his sight had been restored.

All the while they listened to him. Then Paul added that once, when he was praying in the Temple at Jerusalem, God appeared to him and told him to leave Jerusalem for the people there would not believe him, and go instead to preach to the pagans in far-away lands.

At this the crowds burst out afresh, yelling and throwing things. This brought the soldiers running and the tri-

believer in the Lord Jesus and you will be saved and so will all your family.'

Then he washed their wounds and he and all his family were baptised, then they sat down to a celebration meal together.

The next morning the magistrates, afraid that there could be some connection between the earthquake and the men they had imprisoned, sent word to the prison to release Paul and Silas. The goaler gave this news to Paul, but Paul refused to leave.

'Do they think they can treat Roman citizens this way, throwing us into prison without a trial, then sending us on our way!' he declared.

When the magistrates heard this they were appalled to learn that the men they had imprisoned were Roman citizens for they had believed them to be Jews. Immediately they hurried to the prison and begged Paul and Silas to leave.

So they did, and continued on their travels.

•

meeting of the chief priests, for he wanted to know what were their charges against Paul. Then he had Paul brought before them. But the meeting became completely disorganized with the Jews fighting between themselves, and the soldiers took Paul back to the fortress for his own safety.

That night the Lord appeared to Paul and told him 'Have courage. You have testified for me in Jerusalem. Now you must do the same in Rome!'

In the morning the Jews met and hatched a plot to kill Paul. They planned to ask for Paul to be brought for another meeting and they would lie in wait for him and kill him. They vowed not to eat or drink until they had accomplished this. But Paul's nephew, the son of his sister, heard of the ambush and went to the fort with his story.

The tribune did not want any harm to come to the prisoner in his charge, so he arranged for Paul to be escorted to the governor of Judea, a man called Felix, and to ensure his safety he provided four hundred foot soldiers and seventy cavalry.

They left at night and delivered Paul to the governor at Antiatris. The governor read the letter written by the tribune, and arranged for the Jews to bring their case against Paul to him. He listened to their arguments but when Paul mentioned the coming judgement, Felix was afraid and told the Jews he would adjourn the case for the time being. He kept Paul prisoner for two years, often sending for him to talk to him about his beliefs.

Felix was replaced as governor by Festus who was immediately asked by the Jews to bring Paul to trial. He had Paul brought to him, and Paul protested his innocence. Festus was keen to remain on

bune (the man in charge) ordered him to be whipped, for he thought Paul was concealing something and that this would make him speak the truth.

When they had strapped him down, Paul turned to the soldier on duty and asked 'Are you legally entitled to flog a Roman citizen without a trial?'

This stopped the soldier in his tracks. He went to the tribune and told him what Paul had said. Then the tribune himself came to Paul to ask him if this was true and, when he realized that he had chained a Roman citizen, he was worried.

The following day he ordered a

good terms with the Jews so he suggested that Paul should to go Jerusalem for trial.

But Paul insisted. 'I have done the Jews no wrong, if I am to be tried it must be before the court of Caesar.' And Festus was compelled to agree. A few days later King Agrippa and Bernice his sister arrived and Festus told them all about Paul.

'I should be interested to meet him,' said Agrippa, so the following day Paul was brought before the assembled company and Agrippa invited Paul to tell his story.

When Paul had finished Agrippa was very impressed. 'You have almost convinced me to become a Christian like you,' said Agrippa.

'I wish not only you but everybody else here today would be like me . . . except for these chains,' replied Paul.

Then Agrippa and Bernice and Festus talked together and agreed that Paul had done nothing to deserve death or imprisonment, but reluctant to free him without authority they decided to send him to Rome.

Paul, and some other prisoners in the charge of a Roman Centurion called Julius, put to sea. After a few days they ran into a fierce storm, so severe that the captain had to throw the cargo overboard, and then the ship's gear. For several days the storm raged and it seemed as if they could not survive, but Paul told them, 'Don't despair. God has told me that I shall appear before Caesar. We will lose the ship but not our lives. We are to be stranded on an island.'

Just before daybreak on the fifteenth day, Paul said 'Fourteen days you have been worried and not eating. Your safety is not in doubt, eat now,' and with this he took some bread, broke it and ate it, thanking God.

When it was light they saw they were close to an island. The vessel ran aground and began to break up. Some of the soldiers planned to kill the prisoners to prevent them escaping but the centurion in charge would not let them. Some swam ashore, others floated on pieces of wreckage. All landed safely.

The island was called Malta. They stayed there for three months then went on to Rome where Paul taught and preached freely.